Built for Speed

Built for Speed

The Ultimate Guide to Stock Car Racetracks

A Behind-the-Wheel View of the Winston Cup Circuit

by Bob Latford

Running Press

PHILADELPHIA · LONDON

© 1999, 2002 by Running Press
Printed in China

9   8   7   6   5   4   3   2   1
Digit on the right indicates the number of this printing

Library of Congress Cataloging-in-Publication Number 2001094106

ISBN 0-7624-1205-4

Cover photograph by Chris Trotman
Cover design by Matthew Goodman
Interior illustrations by Austin Saylor and Matthew Goodman
Interior design by Rosemary Tottoroto and Matthew Goodman
Photo Research by Susan Oyama
Typography: Adobe Garamond and Helvetica Neue

This book may be ordered by mail from the publisher.
But try your bookstore first!

Running Press Book Publishers
125 South Twenty-second Street
Philadelphia, Pennsylvania 19103-4399

Visit us on the web!
www.runningpress.com

To my late mother, Lois; my brothers Mike and Andy; my wife, Skimp; our daughter, Betsy, whose early years were largely missed as I chased racing around the country; and my grandchildren, Chad, Trent, and Kendal.

To the late Don O'Reilly and Houston Lawing.

To the 29 drivers who lost their lives in the pursuit of the speed and competition in stock car racing's major league in all of its first half-century of practice, testing, qualifying, and racing.

Contents

Preface

While change has been the norm in most aspects of American life, our major sports seem to remain constant, almost as symbols of discipline and die-hard tradition. Football fields are still measured at 100 yards and a 10-yard gain gets a first down. A batter must pass three bases and home plate to score in baseball and there's still only nine innings in a normal game. You still need 18 holes for a round of golf, which is won by the player using the fewest strokes. And most shots through the basketball hoop are still worth two points.

Even in auto racing, victory still goes to the car completing the given distance in the least amount of time. But that's where tradition ends and technology pulls ahead in the dynamic sport of major stock car racing. Virtually every other aspect of this sport, which emerged in the late 1940s following World War II, has changed: the machines, the fans, the rules and regulations, and especially the facilities where the events are held.

Over its history, the cars have changed as rules were introduced to enhance safety: roll bars, fuel cells, fire reduction, safety harnesses, wider and untreaded tires with safety inner-liners. There were other rules designed to produce speed—engine improvements, aerodynamics, revised suspensions. The rules, although vastly more liberal than the original set, are still strictly enforced by an army of inspectors at every event.

Today, Winston Cup cars are virtually hand built from the ground up. While they may resemble the products of American automobile manufacturers on the surface, underneath they are pure racing machines capable of side-by-side and nose-to-tail battles, yet able to protect the driver in a 190-plus mph wreck.

The demographics of race fans has also changed considerably since 1949. Once the exclusive passion of a select fan base comprised of mostly male farmers and laborers, stock car racing now attracts, whether at the tracks or in front of live telecasts that cover every event, a huge cross section of the nation's populace. Now men and women, professionals, college students, and children count themselves among the

The dirt track at Danville Speedway, VA., in the early 1950s.

millions who watch and follow the sport. In fact, auto racing has enjoyed a steady increase in viewers since its inception and is the only major American sport to do so.

In the early years, the distance of a stock car race was a mere 100 miles, 200 laps on the half-mile dirt tracks, which made up the majority of the venues. Gradually the emphasis shifted toward durability as well as speed. The sport saw a move toward bigger tracks in the 1960s and races were lengthened accordingly. During the 1997 Winston Cup season, the average lap was 1.3 miles and each race was contested over an average 400-mile distance.

The facilities that hold the events have undergone the most drastic changes since 1948, the year of the sport's inception. Initially, all the tracks had dirt surfaces with only a slight banking in the turns. Guard rails were typically wooden posts protruding from the top of the turns with planking between them. (Sometimes twine was the only barricade to keep spectators back.) Grandstands, if any, were rickety wooden structures and many fans preferred to watch from their cars parked around the oval or seated in the back of their pickup trucks.

Today race tracks rival other sport's facilities—sur-

passing many—in appearance, comfort, and amenities. But the tracks are distinct from those other sport's arenas. All of the tracks mentioned in this book were built with private funds rather than local tax dollars. Spacious grandstands, some glass-enclosed and air conditioned, some topped with luxurious corporate suites and condominiums, now tower above the tracks of today, all of which are paved. Concrete walls protect the drivers and heavy fences protect spectators from flying accident debris.

In the following pages we will look at the tracks—both present and some of the outstanding ones from the past—which made NASCAR's Winston Cup Series the most highly attended and competitive form of motorsports on Earth. We'll review their physical characteristics, evolution, and history and we'll find the drivers who've been successful at each one and recall some special moments that occurred there. But first, with a feeling that some readers are new to stock car racing's major league and others may not be fully aware of how it all works, we'll guide you through the behind-the-scenes steps involved in Winston Cup racing: how the teams get to a track; how they get in a race; how they get to the finish line.

9

TOP: Dale Earnhardt wins the 1998 Daytona 500. BOTTOM: Dover Downs, 1996.

A bird's eye view of Sterling Marlin's car in the pit.

Behind the Scenes
of Winston Cup Racing

Three elements are necessary to present a major stock car race. The first, obviously, is an acceptable race track on which to run it—one that is racable (can handle side-by-side racing and has appropriate pit and garage facilities, for example), has adequate seating capacity, and meets safety standards. The second is media to cover the preliminaries and the main event—as well as the fans to watch it. The third element is the race teams: The owners, drivers, mechanics, and their machines.

Assembling A Winning Team

Every team starts with an owner—the one who puts it all together. He (or she) must rent, lease, or erect a shop to house the team and equip it with the machines, manpower, and raw materials that enable it to function. The owner hires the driver, assembles a crew, and designates the crew chief who generally runs the competition end of the endeavor and is responsible for the conduct of the crew during each race. Although some of the functions may be designated to a hired crew chief or team manager, the team must get its tractor-trailer, which carries the machinery and cars to the tracks, as well as determine which kind of car it chooses to race and how many it will build. (The team will need at least a primary car and a backup for the super- speedways, interme- diate tracks, short tracks, and road courses which com- prise the circuit.)

In today's racing at- mosphere, each team, if it's to be successful,

must secure sponsorship. The costs are too high to run a racing team without major financial support, and the sport's popu- larity, coupled with fans loyalty to sponsors involved, make such support an effective part of a sponsor's successful adver- tising campaign.

In order to compete in NASCAR events, the team and all of its members must be licensed by the sanctioning body. With the license the team receives a copy of the NASCAR Winston Cup Series Rule Book, which contains most of the regulations regarding procedures, car configuration, how points are awarded, as well as the laws of the sport, including penalties for infractions of those rules. As is the case with "ground rules" in baseball, special circumstances for various tracks may also be spelled out in the Official Entry Blank, which is mailed to each registered team owner and driver a few weeks prior to every event.

  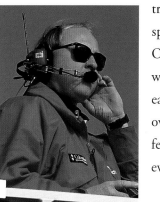

1998 Daytona 500 winning team (LEFT TO RIGHT): #3 car owner Richard Childress, driver Dale Earnhardt, and crew chief Larry McReynolds.

The entry form will also show how much money the track has posted for the race, plus a percentage (about 25%) of the television rights fee paid to the track by the organization or network that's contracted to televise the race. (All Winston Cup races are telecast live because of their popularity.) Also itemized is how the racing and TV moneys are distributed from first through last place, how much has been posted in contingency awards by various manufacturers for those using their products, and the amount of the posted total earmarked for the season's point fund that's built through a surcharge of $125 per $1,000 in racing purse and qualifying money posted by the track. The entry form will also show the pro-rata share of other seasonal awards—Winston Cup Point Fund, as well as Gatorade, battery, oil and similar funds paid out at the end of the season.

The entry blank contains a coupon that must be filled out by the team and list owner, driver, type car, sponsor. The coupon must be mailed along with an inspection fee check to NASCAR. There is no actual "entry fee" in NASCAR events. The fee covers the cost of pre- and post-event inspections. Entries submitted after the deadline are charged a late inspection fee of nearly double.

Teams may either buy or build their cars in accordance with the guidelines of the offical Winston Cup Series Rule Book, which outlines all the pertinent data such as tread widths and wheel base, ground clearances for nose, exhaust pipe, frame rails, and minimum hood, roof and rear spoiler heights. The rules also specify the 350-358 cubic-inch engine displacement, carburetor configuration, and engine placement in the chassis. Safety rules on roll cage configuration stipulate the diameter of

the tubing and minimum wall thickness, and the safety harness for the driver is delineated as to material and type of locking mechanisms. In addition, the 22-gallon fuel cell, with its steel casing and foam rubber interior, the "dry-break" refueling connection, check-valve (to prevent fuel spills if the car turns over), and placement are also discussed in the Rule Book. The sanction body also makes available to the teams exact duplicates of the car's templates, which are used in the inspection process to check compliance with the manufacturers' body dimensions.

With the cars built and tested, manpower assembled, sponsorship in place, transporter stocked with gears, shock absorbers, springs, extra engines, spare wheels, pit equipment, and a plethora of spare parts—and the entry blank filed—the team is ready to head to the event. With the crowded schedule, this usually means the transporter leaves the day before track check-in, while the driver and crew fly in for the first day activities.

Preparing the Equipment and the Facility

Most of the circuit's weekends begin on Friday before a Sunday race. But the NASCAR event officials arrive a day earlier to make their event preparations—to set up their inspection area and equipment and to check the scales that weigh the cars. They must also establish the radio and telephone communications, position the electronic eyes and timing clocks, as well as closely inspect the entire racing portion of the facility—security gates, retaining walls, race control area, and the track surface.

The "tire busters" (an independent crew supplied by the tire

12

Helmets of (LEFT TO RIGHT) Ricky Craven, Kenny Irwin, Terry Labonte, and Bobby Labonte.

company) also come in on Thursday and spend the day unloading their mounting and dismounting ("busting") and balancing equipment. Once set up they must get the allotted three sets of tires inserted with the inner-liner safety shields, mounted on the rims supplied by each team and inflated to the recommended pressures (for both the inner shield and outer tire) and then balanced to assure maximum performance. It can be a full day getting 600 tires ready for an entire entry list of teams (three sets of four tires multiplied by 50 teams = 600) who'll want to go as soon as the track is declared "open for practice."

It is normally pre-dawn when the gates open and the teams' big rigs roll into a track's garage on the opening day of activities. The transporters park according to a set procedure. The defending national champion's rig is always given the first parking spot. (It also gets the first garage space for the season following the title-winning campaign.) For the first four races of each season, the teams are parked according to the final owner points of the prior year with other entries parked next by order of entry receipt. By the fifth race of the season, the trucks are parked and garage space assigned by the current car owner points. (Both driver and owner get the same number of points from a car's performance in every race. So, for example, if the driver gets 100 points, the same is awarded the team owner. If it happened in two races, but two drivers were involved, each driver would have 100 points and the owner would have 200. Thus an owner can have a different total than the current driver for the team, which may occur if a driver is hurt and a substitute is assigned to the car while the primary driver is on the mend.) Owner, not driver, points are used in determinations of parking priority, garage space assignment and starting assignments (top 35) if time trials can't be held.

Once the trucks are parked, the team members may enter the garage area to unload the car and equipment, usually around 7:00 A.M. Their first order of business is to get the car through the mandatory safety and technical inspections. One by one the cars are hand pushed through the inspection line where overall weight and right-to-left side weight distribution are checked (3,400-pound minimum with at least 1,600 of that carried on the right side.) The cars are weighed "wet" with a full load of fuel, oil, and water but without the driver. The drivers are weighed separately, at the start of their season and again halfway through. Drivers weighing less than 200 pounds must add weight to their cars (on the left side) in ten-pound increments to a maximum of 50.

The next inspection step is the height check from roof line, nose, and rear spoiler, ground clearance checks at various points and the application of metal templates to assure that each car's outline conforms to the allowable tolerances for that make and model. The driver area is checked in each machine to look for sharp corners or jagged edges that might injure others. Safety harness and driver-side window nets are examined by the inspection team for signs of wear.

Finally, a compression check is made on the engine to assess compliance with both the compression ratio allowed (12:1) and overall engine displacement of 358-cubic-inch maximum. The test is made on a different cylinder each week to reduce the chance for "hanky-panky" by engine builders. (Prior to the implementation of this procedure, some mechanics were suspected of putting paraffin wax—which melts and is expelled through the exhaust system—in a cylinder to show smaller engine displacement.)

Note: At the tracks where carburetor restrictor plates are mandated to limit speeds (Daytona and Talladega), the teams use their own plates for testing and practice. However, for qualifying time trials and in the race, NASCAR supplies the plate. The sanctioning body also supervises its installation and oversees its removal following the official

Dozens of NASCAR officials are involved in the multiple-inspection process every Winston Cup cars undergoes.

The crew inspects car #77
before the race begins.

activities. The plate used by the winning car is always removed and retired.

If the team passes all phases of the inspection, it's ready to make the initial practice runs when the track is opened. Should they fail, the team members must take corrective action and be re-inspected before they are allowed on the track.

Even though the engines are run in the garage area to get water and oil temperatures up to operating levels—and the rear tires are jacked up and allowed to turn to do the same for the transmission and rear-end grease—the initial laps a car takes on a track are surprisingly slow. The drivers need to get the "feel" of the car and track and report variables to their crews and spotters by the on-board two-way radio, which is mandatory anytime a car is on the track. The pace is gradually increased if everything checks out and lap times—teams deal only in time, not miles per hour (mph)—are compared against the last visit to the track as recorded in each team's notes and also matched against the laps of the competition.

After each run the tires are stuck with a temperature gauge on the inner shoulder, middle, and outer edge. Variances in the readings tell the crew if the car is "tight" and it doesn't want to turn, or is "loose" and turns too much, and if the tire is carrying uniform weight across the width of the tread.

Adjustments are based on the readings. Springs or shock absorbers may be changed, weight distribution can be altered by adjusting the screw jacks on each corner of the suspension. (One full turn of the jack screw will raise or lower that corner of the car one-quarter-inch and transfer the weight carried there from side to side, front to rear, and diagonally.) Carburetor jets may be changed to provide more or less fuel to the cylinders. Ignition timing may be changed depending on what's read from the examination of spark plugs as they are removed and "read" under a magnifying glass by the engine specialists. Rear gear ratios may be changed for better acceleration out of the turns

and to get more top-end speed at the end of the straightaway. All or none of these adjustments may be needed.

One of the three sets of tires allowed each team for practice and qualifying is normally used to get the car set up for time trials. A fresh set of "sticker" tires (the new tire sticker is still on the tread) is then tried on a simulated qualifying run and the third set is held for the actual time trial attempt. (Only if a car has to make a second-round qualifying attempt are they allowed a fourth set.)

Time trials are run for one or two laps depending on the size and nature of the track. Single laps are the norm but two are used on tracks of less than a mile and on tracks where carburetor restrictor plate are mandated, such as Daytona and Talladega.

Qualifying for Pole Position

The order of qualifying attempts is determined by a drawing prior to the first practice session. The driver or crew member may do the drawing. If neither is present, a NASCAR official will draw for them in order of the team's owner points.

Each car is again inspected and must be in the qualifying line when its turn to run arrives. A late arrival is allowed five minutes after the previous car completes its run before being disqualified from the session. If a team has trouble in practice it may be moved to the back of the order by NASCAR officials to allow it time to make repairs.

To "qualify," each car gets a warm-up lap around the track and takes the green flag as it trips the timing light. It breaks the beam again as it passes the line the next time by. The time is translated into speed and both numbers are placed in order among the cars completing their runs. If two (or more) cars turn identical times, the tie is broken by giving preference to the team ranked highest in owner points. At all events the fastest 36 cars are locked into the field in the session.

16

ABOVE: Tire rims ready to be mounted.

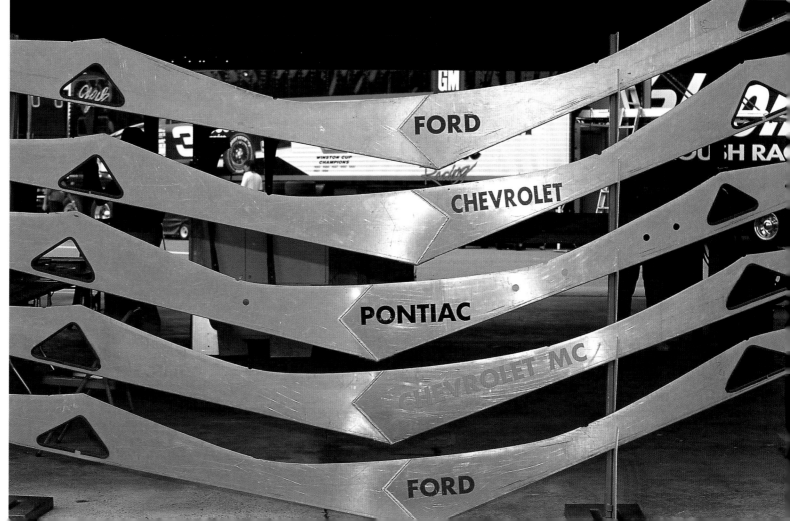

TOP: Sticker tires with
nuts glued in place are
race-ready.

BOTTOM: A rack of the
metal templates used
for car inspections.

After the 25 first-round and 11 second-session qualifiers are set, there may be as many as seven provisional positions added to the rear of the field at every event. The first six spots are assigned to the six car owners with the highest applicable point standings (previous season for the first four races, current standings for the balance of the season) among the top 40.

If all six spots aren't used, those remaining may be assigned to the owners with the highest point standings among the top 40 from the prior season who still aren't in the line-up. The seventh provisional position is available to an owner who has a former Winston Cup Champion in his car, with the most recent former champion having preference. Qualifying time and speed have absolutely no bearing on the provisional or champion's spots. Cars failing to get in the race are awarded descending points behind last place in the race.

So, for example, say 42 cars start, last (42nd) place carries 37 points, and the fastest non-qualifier would get 43rd place's 34 points. If 43 start, last place is worth 34 points, so the top non-qualifier would get 44th place (which carries 31 points.)

If one of the qualified cars crashes beyond repair and is deemed "unrepairable" by NASCAR officials, the team may go to a back-up car that must also pass the usual inspections. The back-up machine would line up in the originally earned position but fall to the rear of the field during the pace and parade laps on race day. Official starting position is ultimately determined when the cars begin to roll for those pace and parade laps even though official timing does not begin until the green flag is displayed.

Once qualifying is completed and the field is set, two important activities can begin. First the teams can select their pit road area for race day with the pole-winning team being given first choice. The team starting second gets the next choice and so on through the back of the field. Most teams would opt for the first pit stall closest to the exit of pit road.

With that spot usually taken by the pole winner, the next option is to select a slot on either side of a pit wall opening to reduce the chances of being blocked in by the car ahead or behind each racecar driver during the always-frenzied pit stops.

At a few tracks there are fewer pits than there are number of starters. In those cases the provisional starters must double up, sharing a pit stall until another team drops out of the event. One of the "double-pitted" teams may move, with NASCAR's permission, to the opened pit area after the other unlucky team officially declares its day is through.

The other final pre-race activity is "Happy Hour," the last practice before the race. This intense 60 minutes follows the other track activity the day prior to the race, usually a preliminary race for another division, like the Busch Grand National or the Craftsman Truck series. It's a time when the teams' cars are in full race trim and the track conditions are most similar to those they can expect on race day. Happy Hour is the time when a car's fuel mileage, tire wear, and handling get the final pre-race test—it is an important day for the racing teams to try their strategies.

Simultaneous display of the red (stop) and black (report to the pit) flags mark the end of the period. Some teams conclude this race simulation with broad smiles from pleasure in their performance. Others return to the garage with furrowed brows and minds racing to find the fractions of a second that can give them a better advantage in the race.

Putting It All on the Line

As race day dawns, the NASCAR officials' meeting is concluding. There, pit road responsibilities, safety car driver and observer, flag men, turn spotters, garage monitors, finish line video crew, scoring supervisors, and race control staff have all

ABOVE: Pole Day ticket for Bristol Motor Speedway.

TOP: A wide angle shot of Lake Speed in his car.

BOTTOM: The #33 car sits in the garage area, wrecked during practice before the Miller 400 race at Richmond, September 1994.

been designated and the ground rules have been reviewed.

After the meeting, inspectors report to their stations where they'll perform the final pre-race safety and technical checks before the event. Only then are the crews allowed to enter the garage area. The team staffs have now been expanded as the weekend members are joined by the race day personnel who'll pit the car. Many of these "weekend warriors" with other full-time professions, occupations, and trades, become jackmen who lift the car so wheels may be changed, tire carriers, wheel changers, or pit scorers who record lap times on race days. Some will assist the full-time team members in making race-day preparations on the car, working from a long list of items to be performed, checked and rechecked, before the car is once again pushed through the inspection process.

Other members of the team—and racing on this level is truly a team effort—are busy moving the diversity of pit equipment to the stall. It's a space that will be laid out with surgical precision every week. Once everything is positioned, the equipment check begins. Air hoses and couplings are checked, attached, and positioned. The tire changers service and test the air guns used to remove and replace the lug nuts. Even the back-up air guns are checked and tested. (Only two guns can be used on a stop. A backup can be brought over the wall only after the primary gun has malfunctioned.)

Likewise, the jackman oils and tests the car jack. Because NASCAR's rules limit pit stops to just one jack, the crew has to be sure it works. But, like the air guns, a back-up may be employed only if the first one fails. The teams' tire specialists check and adjust the air pressures on the sets of tires the team expects to use during the events—usually 10 to 12 sets. Meanwhile, other workers adhere new, "tested" lug nuts, which have been previously spun on a hardened stud to assure clean threads, to the stud holes on each wheel using weather stripping glue,

and gather back-up spare parts—even windshields and sheet metal—in case they're needed. Finally, in the center of their pit, they position the "war wagon," containing compressed air bottles, radio equipment, scoring monitor, video equipment (the top teams all tape their pit stops and review them later, much as football teams study game tapes to find areas where they can improve), extra axles, suspension components, big umbrellas for protection from the elements, as well as laptop computers for calculating fuel mileage and lap times.

With the pit area prepared and the car rolled through its inspections and placed on line, most teams take a lunch break while the driver and crew chief attend their mandatory pre-race roll call meeting. There the track's ground rules, pit road speed limits, and other race-day rules are reviewed. Drivers and crew chiefs may ask for clarification of procedural questions at the gathering and officials may point out potential trouble spots at that track or prior problems that have occurred at the facility as a warning. The drivers are also reminded of their mandatory appearance at pre-race introductions.

Shortly after the meeting, the team scorers and NASCAR staff gather in the scoring stand. Each team supplies a scorer for its car. Scorers have two methods of recording the performance of their charge: a scoring card with blocks for each lap of the race, and a button, which inputs to a computer. On the card each scorer writes the whole-second reading on a flip-type scoring clock positioned usually on the start-finish line. Additionally, each car is fitted with a transponder, that relays the car's passage across the scoring line and feeds the scoring monitors in the control tower, media areas, (radio, TV, press box) as well as each team's pit. Transponder reception cables are also buried in the entry and exit of pit road. In addition, a team of NASCAR officials also monitors these points on the track so pit stops can be factored in should a scoring recheck

ABOVE: Close-up of a tachometer, which drivers use instead of speedometers to judge their speed.

TOP: Pit crews readying for their cars' arrival.

BOTTOM: Bill Elliott's crew working on an engine.

be requested by a team after the event.

While other sports have one ball or puck that's used to score, most races have more than 40 factors involved in determining an event's outcome. Thus a more complex system of scoring is necessary in this sport. Outcomes in stock car racing's major league are so close, some can only be determined by reviewing videotape from the start-finish line camera—especially when drivers race to a caution flag or at the finish. It's a sport measured in thousandths of a second rather than inches.

While the drivers are being introduced to the crowd, NASCAR race officials strategically position emergency equipment around the track and flagmen to their locations. The latter officials can wave a yellow warning flag to alert the drivers of potential trouble in that area but the only official yellow display is the one waved by the official flagman at the start-finish line. At the same time another safety element is being positioned—the team spotters. This group is situated above the track with a sweeping overview of the facility. (On road courses or a track where their view may be hampered by infield obstructions, two sets of spotters may be required.) These crew members are radio equipped and relay safety and traffic information (for example, "clear high," "clear low," "debris low in turn three," and so forth) to their drivers throughout the event and are also monitored by the pit crew.

Knowing the Rules of the Road

With safety equipment, spotters, scoring staff, race officials, caution lights, and radio systems checked and ready, and the drivers secured in their mounts, the starting command is given.

Engines roar as the tachometers (race cars have no speedometers) and gauges spring to life. A final check of tire pressures is made as the oil and water temperatures rise. When they get to operating range, the safety car is instructed to roll off and told how many pace and parade laps will be taken

Modern car jacks, made of titanium and aluminum, are a mere 37 pounds, compared with the old-style 75-pound steel devices previously used to lift the car for tire changes.

before the green starting flag will wave. The same information is relayed to the drivers by the number of fingers shown by the pit road officials and by radio from spotters and crew chiefs who also monitor the NASCAR radio frequencies.

Once the safety car reaches the day's pit road speed limit, it lights up its flashing lights to inform the drivers. At that point, drivers can get a reading from their tachometer and know the revolutions per minute (rpm) they can run on pit road to avoid incurring a speeding penalty. During the warm-up circuits the teams that had to resort to a backup car, or that missed the drivers' meeting or introductions, must drop to the rear of the field. The roll-off sets their official starting position for record-keeping purposes—even though scoring doesn't begin until the green flag waves.

Once the safety car drops off to its position, the snarling, multicolored herd bunches up in rows of two as the green flag is displayed. Right feet stab the throttle, transmissions are shifted to high gear, roaring exhausts bellow and the race is on. Only now can the teams claim their refueling cans at the refueling pumps and take them to their pit stalls.

At the start, passing can occur only to the right until they cross the starting line. After that, they may pass to the right or left of a slower car. (The same holds true on restarts and may result in a "stop-and-go" penalty if violated.) Under the green flag, cars scramble for position as they strive to lead at the scoring line. Each leader gets a five-point bonus and the team leading the most laps gets another five under the organization's point system. A tie for most laps led would result in duplicate five-point bonuses for each leader.

Now the drivers must watch the flagman's other tools as well as listening to their spotter and crew chief while keeping track of traffic and reading the instrument panel. In green-flag conditions, the most frequently used flag is blue with a diagonal orange stripe, which signals drivers to "move over." This flag cues

CLOCKWISE FROM TOP LEFT: Preparing the "Rainbow Warrior's" chariot; tools of the trade; mechanics hard at work under Morgan Shepherd's #1 car; an engine waiting to be installed.

24

the driver to watch his mirror because faster traffic is about to overtake him. A black flag signals a driver to report to his pit for either a rule infraction or trouble with the car that he may not be aware of. If the black flag is ignored after several laps, a black flag with a white "X" on it may be displayed to tell the car involved it will no longer be scored. Ignorance is no excuse here. When a car is black-flagged its number is also displayed at the starting line to inform the cars in the pack who the display is meant to alert. Tower officials also relay the problem to the crew through pit road officials. The spotter may also be informed.

When a yellow flag is displayed it alerts the teams of an unsafe track condition such as an accident, a wet track, or a piece of debris that could cut a tire. As soon at the chief flagman waves the yellow, pit road is closed until the safety car can pick up the leader and get the field in tow. A flagman is also stationed at the entry of pit road who will show a red flag with a yellow "X" on it to inform the drivers that pit road is closed. Anyone ignoring the signal will be penalized. Once the field is under control, the pit road flagman changes his flag to green, indicating that the cars on the lead lap may pit that time by.

Cars that are one or more laps down must wait until the next lap to make their stops. All cars must comply with the pit road speed limit as they enter and leave, whether pitting under a caution or during a green-flag situation.

On a regular pit stop only seven crewmen (including a crewmember who must hold a fuel overflow "catch-can" during the entire refueling procedure) may cross the pit wall and service the car. Under special circumstances, an eighth crewman may be allowed into the service, but only to clean the windshield and/or assist the driver.

When pit stops are completed, the cars return to the track in the order they exit from pit road. This is the time when top crews can consistently gain positions on the competition. (A second gained in the pits may be more than the difference in the fastest-to-slowest lap times of qualifying.) With track cleanup completed, the field is given a "one-to-go" signal at the flagstand, the safety car extinguishes its flashing lights and the lead lap cars line up in the outside column. Cars that are one or more laps down align in the inside column. If lapping on the track hasn't begun at the time of the caution flag, the restart will be in a single file.

ABOVE LEFT: Drivers given the green flag for the start of the NAPA 500, Atlanta Motor Speedway, November 16, 1997.
ABOVE RIGHT: The checkered flag waves over the Atlanta Motor Speedway.

When the leader gets to the halfway point of the race, for example lap 100 of a 200-lap circuit event, the starting stand will display two crossed, furled flags to inform the team that the race is "official," meaning that points and money could be awarded if conditions were to prevent completion of the race from that point on. In odd-numbered lap events (293 laps, 367 laps, and so forth), the signal is given on the lap after the halfway point is reached (lap 147, lap 189).

The flagman may use his fingers to signal the 10 and five-to-go points of the event but will use the white flag to mark the start of the final lap. Of course, it's the checkered flag that concludes the event at the finish line. When the last car has taken the checkered flag, the signal shifts to the simultaneous display of the red and black flags, which signals that the race is over and the track is officially closed.

Adding up the Points

The finish, based on the order of laps completed, determines the points awarded and is the same for all events. The winner receives 175 points, and the values drop by five per position through the top five (so fifth place is worth five more points than sixth). From sixth through 10th place, points decrease by four per position, and from 11th to last place, points drop by three. (This points system is one that I created—at NASCAR's request—in 1974 and has remained unchanged since the start of the 1975 season.) Lap leader bonuses are added to position values and result in the point standings. With the bonus, the race winner will get at least 180 points since he must lead at least on the final lap. He can get 185 if the car lead the most laps of the event.

Upon taking the final flag, the top five cars report to the fuel pumps before going to the inspection area where they will be weighed and inspected. The top two or three, and another car drawn at random, are usually completely inspected after a race, which includes a tear-down of their engines. (The engine of the pole winner is also torn down to assure conformity to the rules.)

The procedures explained in these chapters pertain uniformly to all the tracks where NASCAR's major circuit competes. It's the diversity of the facilities that creates the divergence. The balance of this book will afford you a closer look at these tracks.

ABOVE: The sign for Victory Lane at Atlanta Motor Speedway, where Winston Cup Champions are crowned.

Convertibles come around the bend at the Hickory Speedway in North Carolina, 1956.

Yesterday's Tracks:
Laying the Groundwork

Any look at stock car tracks would be far from complete, and the range of diversity would not be fairly presented, without a glimpse back at the sport's humble beginnings. In this chapter we'll look at some of the people and events present at the creation, and some of the 141 tracks (and two in particular) that have hosted the Winston Cup division and helped pave the way for the sophisticated tracks of today's hottest sport.

From Moonshine Running to NASCAR

Many believe that stock car racing has its earliest roots in illegal whiskey running in the South, during the latter days of Prohibition. (The drink was called moonshine because it was typically delivered at night by car, sans headlights.) Bootleggers would, reportedly, soup up their cars' engines to outrun law enforcement officials. Sometime after the repeal of the Great Experiment in 1933 such evasionary tactics became unnecessary. Fortunately, those mechanically gifted car owners began racing one other. Of course, because their competitions created such spectacles, it wasn't long before they attracted a fan base.

Gradually stock car racing developed into more formal competitions among experimental and Modified stock cars on a variety of tracks that consisted of dirt circuits, road courses, and street races. Unfortunately, many of these early events were haphazardly organized. Drivers had to deal with inconsistent rules, lack of insurance, dangerous conditions, and in some cases,

unethical promoters who ran off with the race purses.

In 1947, in an effort to organize and regulate the sport, William H.G. "Bill" France, a driver in these early days of car racing, and later a top race promoter, served as chairman of a four-day long meeting of drivers, mechanics (including Red Vogt), and promoters that led to the creation of a sanctioning body called the National Association of Stock Car Racing (NASCAR). The new sanctioning body held its first race in 1948, which was open to any kind of stock cars, including those that were "modified" (mechanically altered).

The following year, in 1949, NASCAR formed a new racing division called "Strictly Stock" and opened it to production-line models of "new" (current three years) American-made cars. As the name implied, these vehicles were not allowed to be modified, however the rules did allow for strengthening of the right front wheel. In 1950 this elite division's name was changed to "Grand National" and would become "Winston Cup" in 1972.

An aerial view of the track in Raleigh, North Carolina, July 4, 1956.

ABOVE: Drivers, mechanics, and
promoters, attendees of the
four-day meeting that formed
NASCAR, sit in Daytona's
Streamline Hotel, 1947.

LEFT: A happy Bill France,
having just completed a
good qualifying run at Daytona
Beach-Road Circuit, 1939.

Daytona Beach-Road Circuit

DAYTONA BEACH, FLORIDA
SOUTHERN END OF THE PENINSULA

Size: 4.2 miles
Frontstretch: 2 miles of beach
Backstretch: 2 miles of U.S. A1A

Both unique and historic, the final auto race on the famed course was run in the winter of 1958, to end the area's half century of automobiles battling the clock on the sands along the Atlantic Ocean.

The course's history dates from the turn of the century when auto pioneers like Henry Ford, Louis Chevrolet, and Ransom E. Olds tested their new machines on the tide-packed sandy surface. The tests continued into the mid-1930s when England's Sir Malcolm Campbell set the final 276-mph world record in 1935 in his powerful "Bluebird." Shortly thereafter, the smooth salt of Bonneville, Utah's flats seemed more attractive and less subject to the whims of ocean tides. In fear of losing a major winter attraction, local leaders sought to replace the straightaway speed runs with races. A 3.2-mile course was constructed farther south of the central beach area. (The Dunlawton Avenue or Port Orange beach access ramp was the southern turn and another limestone covered beach-to-land access ramp was situated a mile and a half to the north.) That was the course used for the pre-NASCAR races and the one where local driver Bill France drove and first promoted.

World War II interrupted those events. With peace came the resumption of racing on the course. The end of hostilities also brought a boom to home and motel building in the area. The 1946 and 1947 pre-NASCAR racing events were still run on

ABOVE: An aerial view of the north turn during a Modified race on the Beach-Road Circuit, 1950.

the 3.2-mile layout, but 1948 brought a change. A new 4.2-mile course, employing U.S. Highway A1A as its backstretch and the beach as the front straight, was built farther south toward the less-populated area near the lighthouse at Ponce Inlet. The first NASCAR-sanctioned race was held on a 2.2-mile beach-road circuit, which was part of the 4.2-mile course. (The longer 4.2-mile course was intended for the motorcycle events also held there annually. The short course's north turn proved too hard to maintain and the stock cars became a mainstay of the longer track, which was utilized thereafter.)

The move and new name was an instant hit. More than 60 entries were filed. Some 50 of the pre-war machines, piloted by experienced beach racers and many new faces, lined up for the February 15th event. No time trials were held. The field was arranged in rows, or waves, and sent off at one-second intervals. Local hero Marshall Teague, who opened a gas station in his hometown after returning from flying the "Burma Hump" as an Air Force flight engineer, jumped in front and became the first to lead a lap of NASCAR competition. He led the first 34 laps before Fonty Flock got by him to make the first lead change. Flock was ahead until a spindle snapped, causing the car to flip. Teague was back in front but was promptly challenged by another veteran, Robert "Red" Byron. They raced side by side in the waning laps until a slower machine blocked their path.

30

ABOVE: Sir Malcolm Campbell's Bluebird V, in which he set a new Land Speed Record of 276.82 mph on the Daytona Beach-Road Circuit, 1935.

LEFT: Campbell shows the wear of his Dunlop tires after only two runs.

Tim Flock and Speedy Thompson take the lead during the pace lap of the 160-mile Grand National Race at Daytona Beach, 1956.

Teague, his brakes all but gone, lost momentum as he dove inside the slower car. Byron kept his pace by opting to go outside the obstacle and vaulted his Raymond Parks-owned, Red Vogt-tuned coupe into the lead and became the first NASCAR winner in history. That win in the first of 52 races held in 1948 was one of 11 for Byron who went on to become the organization's first champion.

NASCAR's new car Strictly Stock division was introduced in June of the following year at Charlotte, N.C. The second event of the circuit was held on the Daytona beach-road circuit on July 10, 1949. It featured a 28-car field of '47, '48, and '49 models. It also boasted three female drivers—Sara Christian, Louise Smith, and Ethel Flock Mobley. Ethel, a sister of the Flock brothers, Bob, Fonty, and Tim, drove her husband's Cadillac in the event and created a still-standing record of four siblings competing in a

NASCAR event. As had been the case in 1948, the Byron-driven, Parks-owned, and Vogt-tuned entry emerged the winner and would go on to become the division's first champion.

The site's winter events grew into a Speed Weeks festival. The older model Modified Division, which permitted leeway on engine and car configurations, continued to race over the ever-changing sands. Other divisions were added to the program as they came under the sanctioning body's domain. A Sportsman division was added which allowed fewer changes than the Modifieds. The open-top Convertible division also battled time and tide on the course.

The area's growth again became a problem for the course. Bill France, who retired from driving cars to promote races, saw it coming and started planning for a permanent inland track in the early 1950s. It would finally be done in time for

Daytona Beach racers (LEFT TO RIGHT): Billy Myers, Buck Baker, Jim Paschal, Lee Petty, and Speedy Thompson, 1957.

The checkered flag waves for Paul Goldsmith in the last Grand National Race held on Daytona Beach-Road Circuit, 1958.

June 19, 1949, Charlotte, N.C., drivers race on the Charlotte Speedway during NASCAR's first Grand National race, which would become the Winston Cup.

the 1959 Speed Weeks festivities. The 1958 season opener would be the last on the sands where dunes provided vantage points for spectators to watch the action.

Michigan's Paul Goldsmith was the final new car pole and race winner on the sandy surface in a Smokey Yunick Pontiac. The last combined Modified and Sportsman race was won by Edwin "Banjo" Matthews. He was also that event's first winner when the events moved to the city's new speedway the next season. The final Convertible race went to Virginia's Curtis Turner, who beat out the race's pole winner, Lee Petty.

The promised opening of the new 2.5-mile Daytona Speedway in 1959 ended the era of auto racing on the beach-road circuit. It was colorful and exciting competition on a setting unique in the sport's history. Although the ocean's relentless tides have long since erased the tire tracks, the sports history is deeply imbedded in the white sands of that beach.

Charlotte Speedway
CHARLOTTE, NORTH CAROLINA

Size: .75-mile flat dirt oval

Included, of necessity, is the three-quarter mile Charlotte Speedway where the Strictly Stock division's first race was presented on June 19, 1949. That rutted, dusty oval—crude by current standards—saw a field of 33 cars take the first-ever green flag for a race in what has become the prestigious Winston Cup Series. Glenn Dunnaway, in a '47 Ford, was flagged the winner of the 200-lap race. But a post-race inspection found stiffened rear springs (an old bootleggers' trick) and the car was disqualified for not being showroom quality Strictly Stock, as the rules and initial division name required. The victory was awarded Kansas' Jim Roper even though he had finished second. Although his Lincoln was three laps behind when Dunnaway got the checkered flag, it did pass the post-race inspection.

The Charlotte track was the first of the 164 that would host the new car races with those facilities in 35 of the contiguous 48 states, plus two in Canada.

Gone But Not Forgotten

Not long after the Charlotte Speedway opened, venues for stock car racing spread the width and length of the nation from West Palm Beach, Fla., to Bremerton, Wash., and from California to Maine. Although considered by many a Southeastern sport, only 75 of the 164 tracks—less than half—that have hosted the Series are in the Southeastern part of the country.

The current trend is to build paved, banked superspeedways, but few may realize that these events have been contested on tracks as small as the 0.2-mile oval at Islip, Long Island, and as long as the 4.2-mile Beach-Road circuit in Daytona (the Elkhart Lake road circuit in Wisconsin where Tim Flock drove a Mercury to victory in 1955 was 4.1-miles around). Many of the new tracks are equipped with lights for night races. The first big track to be lighted was the one-mile paved oval at Raleigh, N.C., where they raced in the 1950s. Raleigh's Fairgrounds half-mile dirt oval was the locale for the circuit's final dirt track event run Sept. 30, 1970 with Richard Petty being the last to win on an unpaved track.

Just eight races counted toward 1949's inaugural championship won by Robert "Red" Byron. The most point-awarding events in a season were the 62 held during the 1964 campaign. Of the tracks run that season just Atlanta, Bristol, Charlotte, Darlington, Daytona, Martinsville, and Richmond still host the sport's major league in the dawn of the millennium.

Gone now, victims of commercial development or abandonment, are sites like Hickory (North Carolina) Speedway where Hall of Famers like Ned Jarrett, Junior Johnson, and Ralph Earnhardt (Dale's dad) learned to bang fenders. Ohio's Dayton Speedway is no more but was the 1950 site of the first win by a Ford, driven by Jimmy Florian, who elected to drive without a shirt because of the dusty conditions. Absent now also is the two-mile circuit on the runways of Linden, New Jersey's airport, where the first NASCAR road race was held and won by a British Jaguar—the only time a foreign made car won in the sport—driven by Al Keller. The first Winston Cup start for Richard Petty came on July 18, 1958, on a one-third mile track

35

in Toronto, Canada, where they no longer race, and Bobby Allison first tasted a big-time victory on a similarly sized oval at Oxford, Maine, in 1966. Herb Thomas won one of his 48 victories on a track at Rapid City, S.D., in 1953 and Marshall Teague piloted a Hudson to victory at Gardena, Calif., in 1951, the first time stock cars raced in that state, which now hosts two Winston Cup events annually.

Over the years, the cars and stars of stock car racing's major league have run at 28 tracks in North Carolina, of which only Charlotte and Rockingham still remain, and 15 New York facilities, of which only Watkins Glen remains. The race at the half-mile Gardena track was the first of 14 sites used in the Golden State, which still hosts races at its new Fontana and Sears Point facilities. A dozen tracks hosted the competition in Georgia, with only the remodeled Atlanta Motor Speedway the sole surviving Peach State representative. Tied for fifth on the list are the 10 tracks in Pennsylvania and South Carolina, respectively, with only Pocono and Darlington left to represent their respective states.

Gone from the present-day scene are the circular mile at Langhorne, Pa., and the narrow one-mile oval at Hillsborough, N.C., as well as the classic dirt half-miles at Columbia, S.C., Davenport, Iowa, and Fonda, N.Y. The mile-and-a-half track at LeHi, Ark., no longer throbs to the rumble of the unmuffled

cars, nor does the half-mile Beltsville Speedway in Maryland.

Such change comes with time. The same is true in other aspects of racing. Attrition was high in the sport's formative years. If a third of the starters were running at the end of the early races it was considered good. By contrast, the last two fall events at the now-closed North Wilkesboro, North Carolina Speedway saw every starting car running at the end. Compare that with a 1957 race at the half-mile Asheville-Weaverville Speedway. It was for NASCAR's Convertible division, which existed from 1956 through the 1959 season as a sister series to the Winston Cup, which later absorbed it. The cars were the same, only without roofs. (Many drivers had "zipper" tops they used in Cup races and removed for Convertible contests.) The 26-car starting field for the 200-lap chase had already been thinned by mechanical failures and wrecks before a massive crash on the 181st lap eliminated all but one of the 15 who remained. Curtis Turner managed to squeeze his roofless Ford through and, being the only running car left, enjoyed an uncontested victory.

Some 144 of the 166 tracks are no longer part of the circuit. But from the oldest survivor at Martinsville, Va., to the newest at Chicago and Kansas City, those that remain have risen to showcase the best of stock car racing.

ABOVE: Drivers race on the narrow, one-mile oval at Hillsborough, N.C., 1960. RIGHT: Lighting, crude by today's standards, was an exciting development at the one-mile Raleigh, N.C. oval, the first big track to be lighted, circa 1950.

Part Three: The

Today's Tracks: Built for Speed

In this section we take a close look at the 22 current racetracks where the elite division of NASCAR competes, as well as two important, much-loved tracks that have closed in recent years. Chronologically ordered, all of these tracks reflect the history and remarkable evolution of stock car racing to its modern, technically sophisticated form.

Tracks
of the Winston
Cup Circuit

A wide-angle view of turns No. 1 and 2 at Martinsville.

Martinsville Speedway

MARTINSVILLE, VIRGINIA

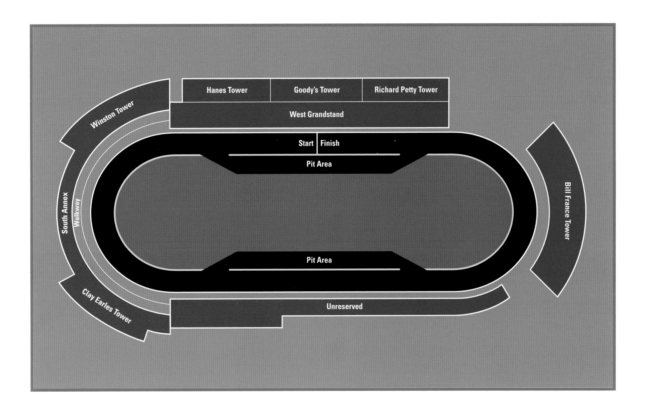

Among NASCAR's Winston Cup tracks, this picturesque oval is unique—not solely for its size, which, at .526 mile in length, makes it the shortest of the currently used facilities. Nor is it unique simply because, at top speeds of only 90-plus mph, it's the slowest track. No, this track's most significant distinction lies in its history.

Martinsville Speedway hosted one of the 1948 races during the sanctioning body's first season—and is the only track still on the Winston Cup circuit that ran races for the 1949 Strictly Stock inaugural season.

Martinsville opened in 1947 as a narrow half-mile oval topped with the rich red clay of the southern Virginia area. The first event there drew a crowd of finely dressed folks who came to the track directly from local church services. They watched the pre-war coupes and coaches battle in the 200-lap chase won under a cloud of dust by Robert "Red" Byron's 1939 Ford. The spectators who stayed to the end left with their Sunday best covered with the same dirt that made driving the track difficult. The following season, the oval hosted one of the first races to be conducted under the newly formed NASCAR banner. Dust control was slightly better than the prior year and the spectators had learned it would be a good idea to change their clothes before coming to the track.

Two years later in 1949, when NASCAR formed its Strictly Stock division for "new" cars, the speedway immediately signed up to host one. Its event ran as the sixth of the eight races that would create the new Strictly Stock circuit's champions. The outcome was the same as it had been two years earlier with Byron claiming the victory. This time he was driving a new Olds 88 entered by Atlanta's Raymond Parks. Their Martinsville performance, along with their results in the other races, led to Byron earning the division's first driving title and to Parks becoming the first car owner champion of the division. (Byron and Parks had also won the same titles in 1948 to

TRACK TACTICS

Drivers need strong low-end torque to get off the turns at this track, which is noted for being hard on gears and fenders. Making brakes last is essential for winning here.

become NASCAR's inaugural champions of any division.)

A second "new" car race, also a 200-lap, 100-mile event, was added to the track's spring schedule in 1950. The distances were maintained through the 1955 season, a year that saw the dust problem finally solved by paving the track. In 1956 both events were extended to 500 laps, 250 miles, and are still run at that length as the track goes into its second half century of operation. This track has long been an innovator. It was the first to landscape the grounds and elected, in 1978, to replace the asphalt turns with more durable concrete. It was years ahead of Bristol and Dover, both of which changed from macadam to cement in the 1990s.

42

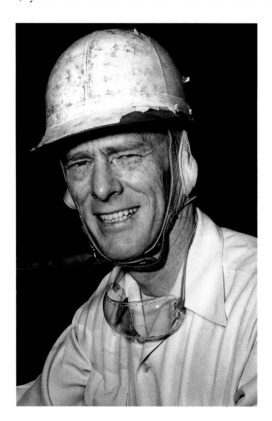

LEFT: Robert "Red" Byron dons a smile at Daytona Beach, circa 1948.

RIGHT: Dust flies on the narrow half-mile dirt oval during the first race at Martinsville, September 7, 1947.

View of the modern-day
Martinsville during the Goody
500, which Bobby Hamilton
won, April 20, 1998.

Lee Petty, runner-up to Byron in 1949 and to Herb Thomas in the 1950 race, didn't break into the track's winners' list until the second race in 1953. He won again the following spring and was the winner there in 1959 after the events had been lengthened. Thus the Petty family name was in the track's record books before Lee's son Richard won there for the first time in the spring event of 1960. When he retired at the end of the 1994 campaign, Richard Petty was a 15-time Martinsville winner.

Other names on the Martinsville winners' trophies include Darrell Waltrip, inscribed 11 times, and Geoff Bodine, four times. The eldest of the New York racing brothers, Bodine had won at the track in Modified and Busch Grand National events

before scoring the first of his four "500" victories in Winston Cup competition there. He's the only driver to have won on the track in three different major divisions of NASCAR racing.

All of the Hall of Fame drivers of the sport have raced at the tight demanding oval. Nearly all of the divisions in the sanctioning body's line-up have battled the dragstrip type straights and hairpin corners. The track has challenged them all. As Cale Yarborough, a five-time pole winner and six-time race winner there, once explained, "It's more difficult to run around Martinsville at 90 miles an hour than to get around Daytona or Talladega at 190. But when you drive at that pretty little track you know you are running in the tire prints of some of the greatest stock car drivers in history."

ABOVE: Richard Petty slows down for a picture at Martinsville, 1977.

RIGHT: Drivers jockey for position in the first turn at Martinsville.

Terry Labonte claims the checkered
flag at the First Union 400, just
seconds ahead of teammate
Jeff Gordon, April 14, 1996.

North Wilkesboro Speedway

NORTH WILKESBORO, NORTH CAROLINA

This tilted oval was built after World War II in the foothills of the Blue Ridge Mountains in North Carolina at a time when the area was known as the "Moonshine Capital of the World." Funds for construction were limited. The bulldozer operator hired to level the site was told to make it as level as possible—"between this rock and the tree down yonder," said Enoch Staley, the track's founder. The money allotted was quickly used up and the track ended up with the first and second turns about 15 feet lower than the third and fourth because of finances.

Despite its uphill backstretch and its downhill run into the other two corners, the track was among the first of the 20 to present a NASCAR race when the sanctioning body was formed in 1948. It was also the venue that hosted the eighth and final "new car" race for 1949's inaugural season of the Strictly Stock division, which became the Winston Cup Series of today.

Six of the 52 races in 1948 were contested on this track's half-mile dirt surface. Red Byron won the first of those six on his way to the first championship in NASCAR history. Other winners at the track that season included Marshall Teague and Curtis Turner—who won three of the races including both in the September double-header.

Size: 6.25 miles • Turn Banking: 14 degrees • Straight Banking: 3 degrees

The first Winston Cup race at the track was run Oct. 16, 1949. A field of 22 cars took the green flag led by pole winner Ken Wagner's Lincoln. He'd earned the top starting spot with a qualifying lap of 57.56 mph. The pole honor was all he would be able to claim for the day as he was overcome by Bill Blair, a High Point, N.C. native, who shoved his Cadillac's nose in front and stayed there for the first 180 laps. But with just 20 of the total 200 laps remaining before Blair could claim the title of first North Wilkesboro Cup winner, his engine went "south." He finished 10th as Bob Flock, eldest of the trio of racing brothers, assumed command of the race for the final laps. He led the field to the checkered flag by 100 yards with Lee Petty taking second in the only Plymouth entered and the only other car to complete the full distance of the day's race.

Before they returned in 1950, the track was extended to a 5/8-mile (.625) oval, the length maintained until it closed, still

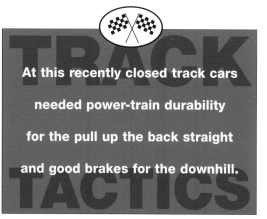

At this recently closed track cars needed power-train durability for the pull up the back straight and good brakes for the downhill.

off-kilter, at the end of the 1996 season. In 1951, the track began hosting two annual events for the new cars and was paved between the 1957 events. The races, which ran for 160 laps, 100 miles, through the 1960 season, were extended to 200 miles for the next three years and, beginning with the 1964 events, were again lengthened to 400 laps, 250 miles.

The most dominant performance in a race at North Wilkesboro was the 1967 spring event. Darel Dieringer had been tapped to drive the yellow Ford fielded by local legend and recently retired driver Junior Johnson. Dieringer showed Johnson's choice driver a wise one by taking pole honors and going on to lead all 400 laps—one of only two times a car has so dominated a race of 250 miles or more. The other was the spring race at the Bristol, Tenn., track six years later when Cale Yarborough led all 500 laps. Interestingly, Yarborough was also driving a Johnson-owned car.

Herb Thomas in the #92 car, kicking up dust at the North Wilkesboro dirt track, circa 1949.

Aerial view of the 6.25-mile oval of North Wilkesboro, nestled in the scenic mountains of North Carolina.

Johnson had been a four-time winner at the track before hanging up his helmet in 1966. He was also ranked second (tied with Bobby Isaac) on the track's all-time pole winner's list with six, even though he didn't drive there for the final 30 seasons it operated. He and Isaac rank behind only Darrell Waltrip's nine poles (six while driving for Johnson) on the track's final all-time list. When the record books closed on the track in 1996, the top name on the "Winners" column was Richard Petty with 15, six of those consecutively scored in the track's spring race from 1970 to 1975.

The 1989 fall race at North Wilkesboro had a bizarre ending. The event had been dominated by the black Chevy driven by Dale Earnhardt. Having led 333 of the 400 laps, Earnhardt was leading the pack to the green flag, which ended the day's 11th and final caution, but had allowed the field to close on his black rear bumper. At the green, and with two laps to go, second-place driver Ricky Rudd tried an inside pass as they went down into the first turn for the final time. Rudd's green Buick and the black Chevy made contact and both cars skidded up the track and into the wall. Geoff Bodine, who hadn't put the yellow-and-white Hendrick Chevy at the front of the field all afternoon, slipped by the wreck and went on to score his first win of the season by leading only the final lap of the race. It was the first time in 18 years anyone had won a race by leading only the final lap.

The last race at the track was run Sept. 29, 1996 and was won by Jeff Gordon. That event mimicked an aspect of the original Cup race in 1949. Ted Musgrave, like Wagner in 1949, was the final pole winner in a race in which he never led a lap. But unlike the '49 event, all of the 1996 starters were still running when Gordon took the checkered flag.

The track was purchased from the founding Staley and Combs families of the Wilkesboro, N.C., area by Bruton Smith and the Bahre family. The track's dates were moved to Smith's new Texas facility and to Bahre's New Hampshire track in 1997. These transfers thus ended an era of racing at North Wilkesboro, which had seen the growth of the sport from the days of "Moonshiners' races" to the modern days of big-budget teams, huge numbers of fans, and live television coverage.

50

LEFT: The North Wilkesboro facility of the mid-'60s.

RIGHT: Driver Darel Dieringer, shown here boasting a win, flanked by Miss Virginia, 1967.

Todd Bodine's #75 car skids sideways as Jeff Burton's #8 car, Derrike Cope's #12 car, and others collide behind him in the fourth turn during the Mountain Dew Southern 500 at Darlington, September 3, 1995.

Darlington Raceway

DARLINGTON, SOUTH CAROLINA

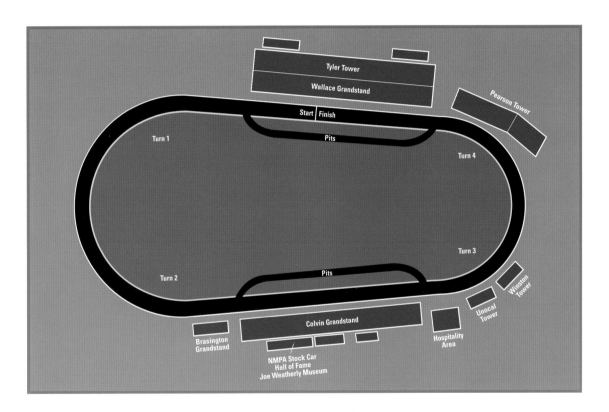

Harold Brasington liked what he saw when attending the Indianapolis 500 in the late 1940s. He believed that a big track, built to race stock cars, would be successful. When he returned to his home in the small cotton and tobacco farming community in Darlington, S.C., he acquired some land and began building what he saw in his mind's eye, much to his neighbors' chagrin. While they scoffed, he methodically moved dirt.

It was a modest undertaking with no engineers or architects to assist in the design—just Harold and a few helpers on bulldozers and other earth-moving equipment. He hadn't been able to talk a nearby farmer out of selling his fish pond, which would have allowed for a sweeping western turn on his track, so he shortened the radius of the western end of it and raised the banking slightly. Even today, it still doesn't match the sweeping eastern turns. Then he paved the track with asphalt, a revolutionary idea at a time when all stock car tracks were dirt.

Harold's then-novel idea to run stock cars—new ones at that—for 500 miles struck locals as an even more bizarre idea than the track itself. It was assumed that a regular car would never be able to last that long. But Harold proved them wrong. To get a field of 75 cars, Brasington enlisted the organizational

---

Size: 1.366 miles • Turns 1-2 Banking: 25 degrees • Turns 3-4 Banking: 23 degrees • Straight Banking: 2 degrees

TRACK TACTICS

At this track drivers need to compromise springs and shocks to accommodate the differences in turns.

skills and promotional talent of Bill France, a young man from Florida who'd just started a stock car racing group called NASCAR.

Together they organized the race, the "Southern 500" to be held on Labor Day 1950. A purse of $25,000 was posted and it took two weeks to qualify the field. Driver Curtis Turner was the first pole winner, pushing his Olds around the mile-and-a-quarter egg-shaped track at an average of 80.034 mph. Some days later Wally Campbell turned a lap of 80.4 mph, becoming the event's fastest qualifier, but he had to start 60th, outside of the 20th row, in the three-wide, 25-row-deep field. (The first World 600 at Charlotte in 1960 also had a three-abreast starting field.) Campbell started behind Johnny Mantz's Plymouth,

the slowest qualifier at 73.460, who'd gotten his berth in the time trial a few days earlier.

The naysayers of Harold's idea had been partially correct, though. The strain of the banked turns and race distance took a toll on the field. By 50 laps the wisdom of Mantz in picking a lighter Plymouth to go against the heavier Oldsmobiles, Lincolns, Cadillacs, and Mercurys proved correct. While the heavier machines broke suspensions and blew tires, Mantz was cruising to a nine-lap victory over Glenn "Fireball" Roberts' bulky Oldsmobile and became the first 500-mile winner, the first paved track champion and the first super speedway victor in stock car history, all in his first stock car attempt, which he completed in six hours, 38 minutes.

ABOVE: Drivers on the start line at the Southern 500, 1950.

OPPOSITE PAGE, LEFT: Jeff Gordon zooming into turn No.3 at the Southern 500, August 31, 1997.

OPPOSITE PAGE, RIGHT: Dale Jarrett takes first place at the TranSouth Financial 400, March 27, 1998.

The track was extended slightly in 1953 and rebanked to its present configuration in 1969. In 1956 they added a spring race to the schedule, the "Rebel 300," held on Confederate Memorial Day for the NASCAR Convertible Division. The ragtops were replaced by roofed cars after the 1962 season and the race has been run as part of the Winston Cup series since.

Herb Thomas drove a Hudson to victory in 1951's "500" by topping an 82-car field that featured 16 different makes of cars. That race still holds the record in NASCAR's major league for both size of the field and the wide variety of car models competing. Thomas repeated his 1951 conquest in 1954 to become the era's first two-time 500-mile winner and added a third the following Labor Day. In 1997, Jeff Gordon became the first driver in Southern 500 history to win the race three straight times, and extended his run a year later, to be the first driver in NASCAR history to win four consecutive editions of any super-speedway event.

Over its long and storied history, Darlington Raceway, deemed by many as the most demanding on the circuit, has seen many other drivers excel. Fireball Roberts, second in the inaugural, won both the spring race and the Labor Day classic twice. (The 1963 edition of the Labor Day Classic was never slowed by a yellow flag.) By the time he retired, David Pearson had won 10 times on the track, one more than Dale Earnhardt as the circuit entered the 1998 campaign. Seven of Pearson's wins and six of Earnhardt's came in the spring event. But both trail retired Cale Yarborough, who started his career by crawling under the fence to drive while still underage. The stocky South Carolina resident and subsequent team owner won the Labor Day event five times before climbing out of a driver's seat for the last time.

To accommodate grandstand expansion, the track, now owned by International Speedway Corporation and a sister facility to Daytona and Talladega, had to flip the track, moving the start-finish line to what had been the backstretch. But that didn't alter this demanding facility, justly titled "Too Tough to Tame."

ABOVE: It's only smiles for Johnny Mantz, winner of the Labor Day Southern 500, 1950.

RIGHT: Neil Bonnett's pit crew in action during the Southern 500, 1985.

Jeff Gordon takes his first win of the season at the Pontiac 400, March 3, 1996.

Richmond International Raceway

RICHMOND, VIRGINIA

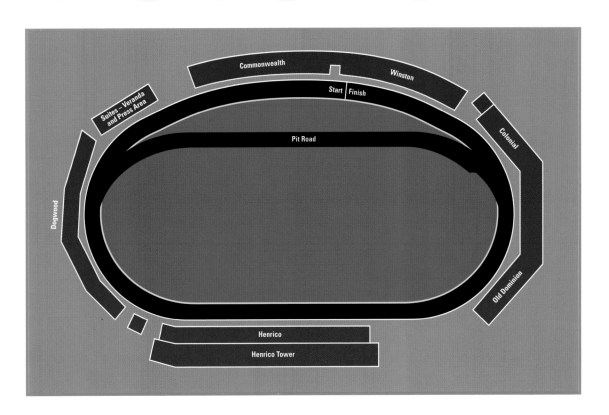

Virtually no facility, among the many that host NASCAR's biggest division, has undergone the metamorphosis seen at the track situated on the State Fairgrounds in Virginia's capital. Drivers who'd raced there on a rough dirt half-mile oval in 1953—the first season it presented the division that became Winston Cup—would not recognize the modern track that towers above the site today.

Wide and smoothly paved, this brilliantly lighted track is nearing the 100,000 seats needed to accommodate fans' requests. It is also unique in having seen three second-generation drivers and one third generation—win major events here.

Originally referred to as "Strawberry Hill Raceway," the track was considered so bumpy that some drivers claimed it got its name from having the fruit picked off it the evening before they raced. Buck Baker, the Charlotte, N.C. bus driver-turned-race car driver, was the pole winner for the April 1953 inaugural event, with a speed of only 48.5 miles an hour on his qualifying lap. Lee Petty, patriarch of his racing family, piloted his Dodge to victory and became the first racer to win on the track. Petty, who would go on to become a three-time series champion and winner of the 1959 inaugural Daytona 500, would see his son

Size: 0.75 miles • Turn Banking: 14 degrees • Straight Banking(front): 8 degrees * Straight Banking(back): 2 degrees

Richard become a 13-time Richmond winner and his grandson, Kyle, add his name to the facility's winners' list.

A second race was added at the track in 1958 with Lee Petty almost being the winner of both inaugural events. He finished second only to Alfred "Speedy" Thompson—the only other driver to complete all 200 laps of the event.

Passing seasons saw changes to the track and its events. The races were lengthened to 250, 300, 400 laps. A few were 500 lappers. The track was extended to .625 miles and paved in the late 1960s. Before the facility was razed and reconfigured in 1988, it was listed as a ".542-mile oval hosting 400-lap events."

Following 1988's spring event, won by Alabama's Neil Bonnett, Richard Petty climbed aboard a bulldozer and ripped up a portion of the asphalt track surface. Petty's planned bulldozing stint resulted in the complete demolition of the old track. What emerged in its place remains as the present-day 3/4-mile track—designed by Charles Moneypenny, who'd also engineered the construction of the Daytona, Michigan, and Talladega tracks—featuring an eight-degree bow in the front stretch and the 14-degree banking in the turns.

The winningest driver in Richmond history is Richard Petty with 13. His victories included a string of seven in a row. From the fall race in 1970 through the two in 1973 no one else was honored in the track's victory circle. Over the sport's history only Darrell Waltrip's seven consecutive Bristol wins can match Petty's Richmond achievement. Bobby Allison had won seven times on the old Richmond facilities, second only to Petty's 13. Allison's son Davey, driving a Robert Yates owned Ford, would become the first to win on the new layout as he beat Dale Earnhardt's black Chevy to the line by three seconds in the 1988 inaugural.

Lights were added to the Richmond track's arsenal of features to accommodate television coverage, and in 1991 the fall race was run under them for the first time. They shined on Harry Gant as he won not only the Saturday night Winston Cup battle but also triumphed the previous evening in a 200-lap Busch Grand National division race to become the first night winner at the

A wide angle view of Richmond International before the start of the Exide 400, September 6, 1997, with F-16 fighters flying overhead.

track. His Cup victory was the second of four in a row that the North Carolina driver would win that September. He'd won the week before at Darlington and would win at Dover and Martinsville the following two weeks.

The lights were shining, too, in September 1997, when Dale Jarrett scored his first Richmond victory. In doing so he joined the site's victory list that includes his father,

TRACK TACTICS

Handling is key here on the fastest of the short tracks. Having a good gear selection helps drivers in getting off the tight second turn.

Hall of Famer Ned Jarrett, a winner on the dirt track that was there in 1963. Thus the Jarretts, along with the Allisons and Pettys, share the honor of having more than one generation of drivers who were victorious at Richmond—the only track on the present circuit that's the same length (3/4-mile) as the Wilkinson Boulevard Speedway in Charlotte, the site of the division's first race back in 1949.

LEFT: Terry Labonte poses in victory lane after claiming first place at the Pontiac 400, June 6, 1998.
RIGHT: Miss Firebird presents the Richmond 300 winner's trophy to Ned Jarrett, September 8, 1963.

A glimpse of the low-tech pits of earlier days at Richmond International.

Dale Jarrett and Terry Labonte coming out of the S's during the Bud at Watkins Glen, August 1996.

Watkins Glen

WATKINS GLEN, NEW YORK

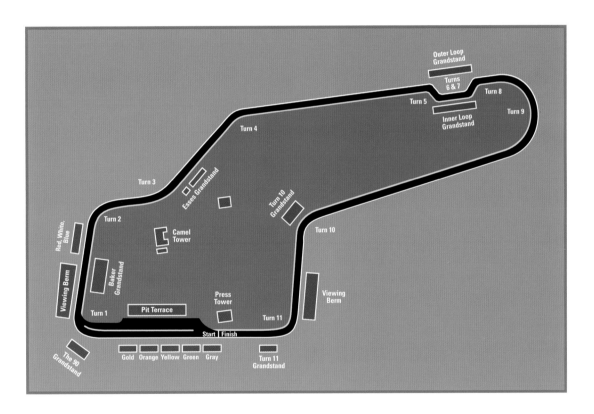

The arrival of NASCAR's major division at the scenic Watkins Glen road course in 1986 signaled the beginning of an annual event that continues today. It was not, however, the first time Winston Cup racers had raced the same track made world famous by the Grand Prix Formula One races. The division's initial race at the serpentine facility had come 29 years earlier, in 1957. But the 1986 event was instrumental in revitalizing not only the track but the economically depressed area in the Finger Lakes region of New York.

This area's racing history dates from the time sports cars battled through the streets of Watkins Glen. As that became hazardous to competitors and the public alike, the races were moved to a 2.3-mile permanent course at the present site in 1956. The following season, on Aug. 4, the NASCAR banner first appeared at the complex. It was NASCAR's 35th event of a 53-race season. Twenty cars were on hand with veteran Buck Baker of Charlotte driving his Chevrolet to pole honors with a qualifying lap of 83.06 mph. Baker was destined to lead every lap of the 44 involved to claim a half-second victory over the Ford piloted by Fireball Roberts. It would be the sole road course win of Baker's career, which included 46 victories, two championships, and induction into the Hall of Fame.

Size: 2.45 miles • Turns: 11 (7 right, 4 left)

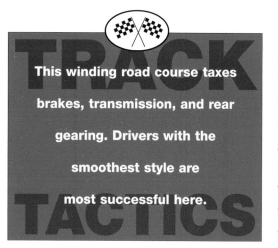

This winding road course taxes brakes, transmission, and rear gearing. Drivers with the smoothest style are most successful here.

Common at the time, but unheard of now, the same day saw another NASCAR road race. It was run on a nine-tenths-of-a-mile layout at Kitsap County Airport in Bremerton, Wash., where a driver named Rufus "Parnelli" Jones would win his first NASCAR race. The Ford-mounted Jones would go on to Indy-500 fame but would win three more times under the NASCAR banner, including 1967's Motor Trend 500 at California's Riverside Raceway road circuit.

Following the 1957 race at "the Glen," the NASCAR stalwarts didn't return to the site for seven years. But they were back to again challenge its hills and curves in 1964 as part of the series' "Northern Tour," a group of summer races held at tracks in the nation's northeast. The cars and stars of stock car's major circuit had raced four days earlier at the one-fifth-mile oval at Islip, Long Island (and would race two days after Watkins Glen at New Oxford, Pa.) as part of the 1964 season's division record 62-race schedule. The race was set for 66 laps over the 2.3-miles. Texas' Billy Wade, in a Bud Moore Ford,

elevated the division's time trial record by nearly 20 mph as he took pole honors at 102.22. Wade went on to win the event, leading 41 laps, as he took a six-second victory over Dodge driver LeeRoy Yarborough. The sophomore Wade had won the three prior events before this one, including a race a week before at Long Island's Bridgehampton road circuit, to become the first driver in the division's history to win four consecutive races. Tragically it would prove to be Wade's final triumph. He died testing tires at Daytona the following January.

In 1965, the teams were back and had a third face beaming in victory lane. Transplanted Californian Marvin Panch drove the Wood brothers' Ford to a victory over Ned Jarrett in the 1965 Glen stop after time trials were rained out and the field aligned by point standings.

Following Panch's victory, the area's terrain didn't echo with the roar of stock car engines again until 1986—19 years after they had last resounded across its lush greenery.

When the circuit returned they found the course extended to

Drivers queued up behind the pace car during the Bud at the Glen.

A dramatic crash that proved fatal for J. D. McDuffie when his Pontiac landed on Jimmy Means' Pontiac in turn No. 5 during the Bud at the Glen, August 11, 1991.

2.428 miles as Tim Richmond jumped the pole speed to 117.563 mph and went on to a second-and-a-half victory over Darrell Waltrip and the rest of the 36-car field. The crowd attracted by the circuit's return was the site's largest since the last U.S. Grand Prix had run there six years earlier. The race has subsequently grown to be the largest sports spectator event in the Empire State.

Following Richmond's 1986 win, the next four seasons saw Rusty Wallace and Ricky Rudd winning alternately. Their pattern was stopped by Ernie Irvan, like Panch a California transplant, who won the race in 1991. Irvan's triumph was marred by tragedy when veteran driver J. D. McDuffie was fatally injured when he wrecked going into the turn at the end of the 2,600-foot-long backstretch. As a result, track officials altered the straight by creating a chicane (consecutive right and left hand turns), which slowed the cars before they reached that right-hand, down hill corner. The alteration extended the track to its present 11-turn, 2.45-mile configuration.

Although Richard Petty can claim six road racing victories among his 200 triumphs, none of them were won at this track.

None of his father, Lee's (one of the 1957 participants here) 54 wins were ever achieved on a road circuit. But in the rain-shortened 1992 Winston Cup race held at this course, Richard's son and Lee's grandson Kyle finally placed the famed racing family's name in the track's record books with a victory. For the three years after Kyle Petty won, the only name on the events' pole or winners' trophies was Mark Martin. The slight Arkansas native took qualifying and race honors each year.

When the Winston Cup made its 1957 debut, an 8-year-old kid named Geoff Bodine from nearby Chemung, N.Y., had climbed a tree along the backstretch to watch. What he saw led him to a racing career with pole honors for the 1988 Winston Cup race at Watkins Glen. Eight years later he was being honored in the track's 1996 winners' circle as the newest Winston Cup driver to triumph at this storied facility.

The next season, the annual stop at Watkins Glen resulted in Jeff Gordon completing his racing resume with a road-course victory there on his way to his 1997 and second Winston Cup championship.

ABOVE: Geoff Bodine celebrating his victory at the Glen, 1996.

Action in the pits at Watkins Glen.

Richard Petty's battered Dodge during the
Winston Western 500 at Riverside, 1975.

Riverside International Raceway

RIVERSIDE, CALIFORNIA

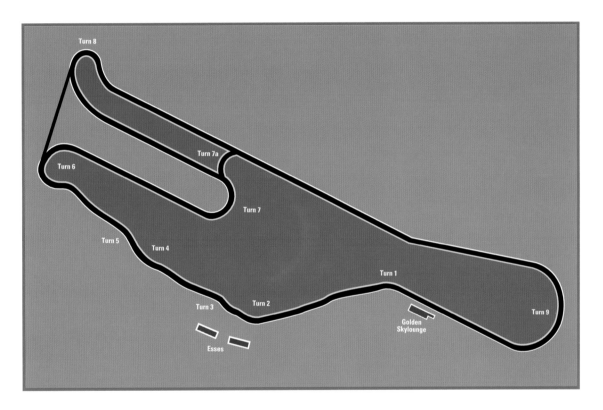

From 1958 until its 1988 closing, the serpentine Riverside International Raceway hosted 47 races for NASCAR's major league circuit. The twisting nine-turn track honored 19 different drivers in its victory lane during the period. The facility, situated just 50 miles from the population center of Los Angeles, hosted each season's opening events from 1970 through 1981 and concluded the annual campaign from 1981 until its final event of 1986.

The southern California facility produced some unusual NASCAR winners and a few regulars scored firsts on its S-turns and demanding switchbacks. Dan Gurney and Mark Donohue, both notable road racers, scored their only NASCAR wins there. Indy car star A. J. Foyt won there in NASCAR competition as did Parnelli Jones, another driver who gained national fame for his feats in the Memorial Day classic in Indiana. The track also saw California's Winston West driver Ray Elder, the "Flying Farmer," defeat the East Coast stars twice. In the 1983 races, Bill Elliott and Ricky Rudd both scored the first victory of their Winston Cup careers on the track to mirror the accomplishment turned in on the track by Tim Richmond the previous season. During the 1979 season, Dale Earnhardt earned the first pole position of his illustrious career in Riverside competition.

Size: 2.62 miles • Turns: 9 (4 left, 5 right)

If you want to collect some money on NASCAR trivia, ask your friends to name the first driver to win four consecutive 500-mile NASCAR races at a track. You can collect if they fail to name Dan Gurney at Riverside Raceway. The former motorcycle racer, who went on to fame in Indy cars, sports cars, Formula One and now as a team owner, was the winner of four of the 500-mile races at the track from 1963 through 1966. Parnelli Jones broke the string with his 1967 triumph, but Gurney returned the following season to get his fifth victory in the six times the event was held—a record that remains unbeaten in any other 500-mile race at any of the circuit's tracks. Gurney won the 1963 event in a Holman-Moody Ford, but scored the next three in a Ford fielded by the Wood brothers' team from Virginia. Jones was in a Wood car when he broke the Gurney streak, but Gurney was back in Wood's car the next time to give the family operation a string of five consecutive 500-mile victories here.

The Winston Cup events at Riverside have known tragedy, too. In 1964's "500," Joe Weatherly, the two-time and defending Series champion, died in a turn-six accident. The former motorcycle racer was the first driver to die in competition while defending the title. Two years later, talented newcomer Billy Foster would suffer fatal injuries while practicing for the event. A third name was nearly added to the list on the 94th lap of 1982's season ender. Terry Labonte, in a Billy-Hagan owned Buick, slammed his car into the end of a concrete wall outside the 180-degree turn nine. The front of the car was torn off and most feared the worst. However, other than severe facial

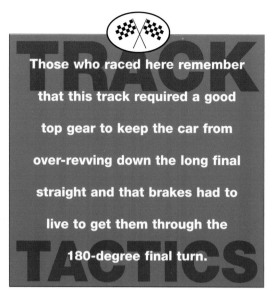

Those who raced here remember that this track required a good top gear to keep the car from over-revving down the long final straight and that brakes had to live to get them through the 180-degree final turn.

cuts, the Texas driver escaped from the wreckage and was able to walk onstage at the awards banquet the following month to accept his third-place Winston Cup Point Fund check to the thunder of a standing ovation.

Eddie Gray, from Gardena, Calif., won the first NASCAR event at the track in 1958. Thirty years later Rusty Wallace was the track's final NASCAR winner. Between those two the most common name on the track's list belongs to six-time winner Bobby Allison. Just one victory behind Allison are Gurney, Richard Petty, and Darrell Waltrip with five each. Parnelli Jones was the 1958 pole winner with a speed of 85.57 mph. The final pole was earned at 118.484 mph some 30 years later by Ricky Rudd.

The big Riverside NASCAR races were run at 500 miles from 1958 through 1977 and then reduced to 500 kilometers, or 312 miles. A second event, a 400-mile chase, was added to the track's schedule in 1970, but was similarly truncated to 400 kilometers, 249 miles, in 1977. Those distances were maintained until the track gave way to industrial development and ceased operations altogether a decade later.

Left now are the memories of the drivers who raced there and the fans who gathered to watch stock car road racing in the dusty desert of southern California. Area race fans who wish to rekindle their affection for the stock cars turning right as well as left must now journey nearly 500 miles north to the Sears Point track or diagonally across the country to Watkins Glen. But if they can suffice with watching racing with left turns only, they'll have a mere 20-mile drive to Roger Penske's new California Speedway oval.

Darrell Waltrip in the winner's circle after the Warner W. Hodgdon Riverside 400, June 8, 1980.

72

Cars twisting and turning through Riverside's famous S-shaped circuit, 1975.

Drivers queued up for racing at Daytona.

Daytona International Speedway

DAYTONA BEACH, FLORIDA

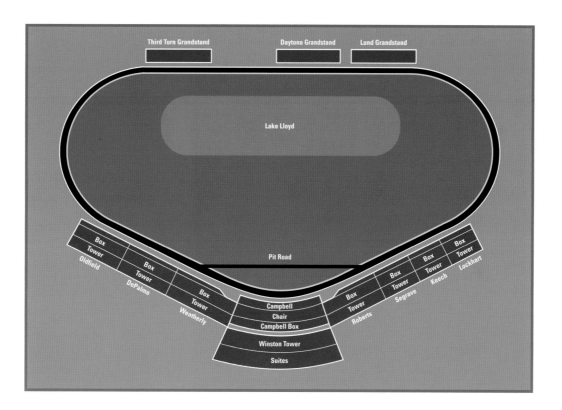

The Daytona Beach area had a long history of motorsports before the 1959 opening of the Daytona International Speedway. In the early 1900s, on the hard-packed sand of the beach on Florida's eastern coast, car racing was a popular winter activity. The next three decades saw more runs as automotive pioneers sought out the beach front as a site for speed record runs, which culminated in 1935 with the 276-mph speed record set by Sir Malcolm Campbell.

The whims of the tide and unpredictable offshore winds led to the demise of time trial racing on the beach. To replace the attrac-

tion, local Daytona Beach officials decided to present their own races on a 3.2-mile beach-road circuit and continue the relationship between the area merchants and motorsports.

The first few tries were less than successful. Then came Bill France, a driver in the early races, who undertook promoting as well as competing in the events. He won a couple of them before World War II brought a halt to racing.

When hostilities ended, racing resumed. By 1946, cars were again battling the shifting sand. Late 1947 witnessed the creation of NASCAR. The organization's first sanctioned race was run in February 1948 on a 2.2-mile course that was located south of

---

Size: 2.5 miles • Turn Banking: 31 degrees • Straight Banking: 3 degrees * Tri-Oval Banking: 18 Degrees

the central beach area. The following year the sanctioning body formed the Strictly Stock division, which held its second race on a new 4.2-mile beach-road course.

Postwar growth along the beach led France to seek another venue. His search led to selection of a cypress swamp west of town near the old World War II Naval Air Station and to the creation of the two-and-a-half mile oval with a bulging front stretch that gave the track a unique shape. The facility's sweeping turns tilted up at 31 degrees and towered five stories tall. The 18-degree slope of the start-finish line assured high speeds.

In February 1959, the racers gathered at the new facility unsure of what lay ahead. They'd never seen such a track—big, wide, and fast. When the dust from preliminary activities had settled, they found North Carolina's Bob Welborn as the track's initial pole winner at 140.121 mph but Pontiac pilot Cotton

TRACK TACTICS

Aerodynamics are the key at this track, but the driver must look well ahead to miss the trouble that typically comes up so quickly. Drafting ability can often overcome lesser horsepower.

Owens was the fastest qualifier at 143.198. Darlington, previously the fastest oval, paled with its 1958 top speed of 117. A field of 59 cars took the track's starting signal for the first Daytona 500. It would be a chase that would end in a dramatic photo finish between Lee Petty's Oldsmobile and the Thunderbird piloted by Iowa's Johnny Beauchamp. Three days of examining finish-line photos and newsreel footage resulted in Petty being declared the winner of the inaugural—and caution-free—event.

Just as the winter event had been moved from the beach to the speedway, a July fourth race was moved from a North Carolina track to the new Florida facility. Local hero Fireball Roberts took both pole and event honors in the first running of the Firecracker 250. That race was extended to 400 miles with the 1963 running and became a night race when it ran under the track's newly installed lights in 1998, although the track was

76

Bill France, Jr. on a compactor, laying the groundwork for the Daytona International Speedway, 1958.

77

ABOVE: Janet Guthrie with her Chevrolet in 1977, the only woman to ever race in the Daytona 500.

LEFT: The last lap of the first Daytona 500 held in 1959, in which Lee Petty was declared the winner.

forced to postpone its running from July to October because smoke from rampant wildfires limited driver visibility.

While Lee Petty's triumph in the track's inaugural 500 place it atop the track's winners' listing, the family's name was added there most frequently by Lee's son Richard. The second-generation driver won the 500 an unprecedented seven times, the summer event three times, and took one of the 500's qualifying races for a track total of ten victories in Winston Cup events. Including all stock car races at Daytona, the biggest winner is Dale Earnhardt with 29 in points races, qualifying heats, and other events. Yet the seven-time Series champion entered 1998 still looking for his first Daytona 500 win, despite four 2nd-place finishes in the sport's biggest race. He finally got the victory in the 1998's edition.

Two of Petty's races were outstanding. One he won and one he did not. The 1976 edition was a thriller. It boiled down to a shoot-out between Petty and arch rival David Pearson. In the final 100 miles only Benny Parsons, other than Petty and Pearson, was able to lead a lap, and he led just one. Petty's Dodge was ahead of Pearson's Mercury as they passed under the white flag to begin the final lap. Exiting turn two, Pearson slipped by, but Petty pushed the Dodge ahead again as the duo entered the third turn. Pearson tried to go low as the two cars exited the four turn for the final time but they touched. Both cars lost traction in the short chute between the fourth turn exit and the finish line. They went spinning, slamming into the concrete wall and back across the track. Petty's mount stalled in the grass but Pearson had popped his clutch and kept the Mercury's engine going. Pearson was able to nose his mashed machine across the finish line to victory while Petty's doomed Dodge sat still, just yards from the magic stripe, and never finished the last lap.

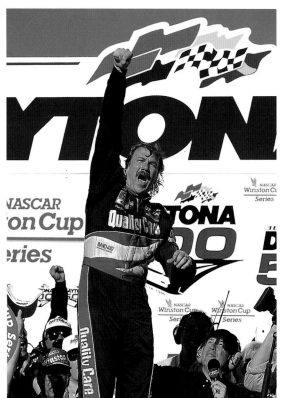

He wound up second.

Three years later the "500" was to be the first race telecast live on CBS. A snowbound eastern half of the country tuned in and what a race they saw. Although the race got off to a slow start—the first 16 laps were run under a yellow flag to finish drying the track—the action quickly heated up. Donnie Allison, driving Hoss Ellington's Olds, and Cale Yarborough, piloting a similar car for Junior Johnson, battled for the lead early before tangling out of the second turn and spinning through the muddy grass along the backstretch. They both recovered and got back in the fray. Working through the traffic like masters, they made their way back to the front by half way. As the laps waned, the two were dueling for the lead again. Allison had his maroon mount slightly ahead as the two took the white flag. As they had earlier, the two cars made contact as they fought for position on the backstretch. Again both went spinning with Yarborough's Olds slapping the backstretch wall and Allison ramming nose first into the third-turn barrier. Both cars ground to a halt on the infield apron. Tempers flaring, they both exited their machines and a fight ensued. Bobby Allison brought his Ford to a halt near the disabled cars to check on his brother and was also involved in the battle.

While the fans and cameras were focused on the fisticuffs, Richard Petty, who had been holding down third place, drove past the melee and on to a one car-length victory over Darrell Waltrip. A.J. Foyt took third with Donnie Allison and Yarborough fourth and fifth, respectively.

It was the sixth of Petty's seven wins—and one he did not expect—in the race which has seen Welborn's initial pole speed upped to more than 210 mph by Bill Elliott in 1987 before the carburetor plates or "restrictor plates," used here and at Talladega, curtailed top speeds.

ABOVE: Dale Jarrett celebrating victory at the Daytona 500, 1996.

A shot from the infield of the high-rise grandstands at Daytona

Start of the Coca-Cola 600,
May 25, 1992.

Charlotte Motor Speedway

CONCORD, NORTH CAROLINA

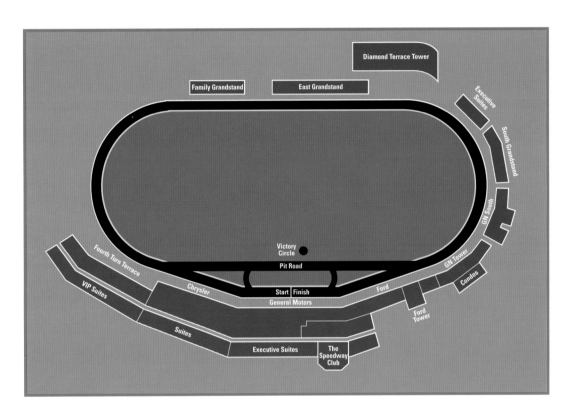

When it opened in June of 1960, Charlotte Motor Speedway was the fourth "super-speedway" (a high-banked track of a mile or more in length) to arrive on the circuit. It joined Darlington, which opened in 1950, Daytona's facility that had come on board the previous season, and a short-lived 1.4-mile track in Hanford, Calif. At a mile-and-a-half in length, Charlotte was unique. Its truncated tri-oval with a double-dogleg frontstretch was also different, as were its corners with their 24-degree bankings, a modest variable to the lower slopes of the turns at Darlington, but considerably less than the steep 31-degree-turns at Daytona.

Not only was the track physically unique, the event held there was distinctive, too. At a time in the sport's growth, when a 500-mile race was thought to be a grueling test of man and machine, the track's founders, Curtis Turner and Bruton Smith, announced their opening event would run 600! The rewards would compensate for the skill and endurance required. The posted awards for the 600-mile grind was $100,000, an unheard of sum in 1960. Turner (a driver himself) and Smith, concerned that attrition would thin the field, chose to start 60 cars, 20 rows at three abreast. Their apprehensions proved right. Wrecks

Size: 1.5 miles • Turn Banking: 24 degrees • Straight Banking: 5 degrees

and mechanical woes thinned the field and failure of the hastily laid asphalt complicated the problems.

The tracks inaugural pole winner, Fireball Roberts (133.904 mph), was among the early casualties, sidelined by one of the day's numerous crashes before the halfway point. With Roberts gone (his Pontiac had led 116 of the 191 run before his crash), the man to beat appeared to be Georgia's Jack Smith, also piloting a Pontiac. Smith's black and maroon mount had built a five-lap lead on the field before a piece of the broken asphalt flew up and punctured his gas tank. Frantic work by his crew, led by Bud Moore, failed to staunch the leak. Watching helplessly, Smith and Moore saw their advantage disappear as the laps waned. Joe Lee Johnson, piloting a Paul McDuffie-owned Chevrolet, swept into the lead

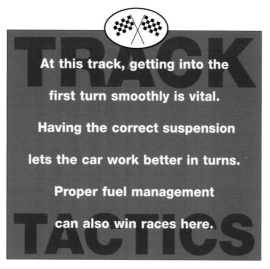

TRACK TACTICS

At this track, getting into the first turn smoothly is vital. Having the correct suspension lets the car work better in turns. Proper fuel management can also win races here.

and went on to a four-lap victory over fellow Chevy chauffeur Johnny Beauchamp. Johnson became the winner of the track's inaugural event and NASCAR's first 600-mile race winner. Beauchamp ended the day with the distinction of being first runner-up in both the inaugural Daytona 500 (to Lee Petty) and the inaugural Charlotte Motor Speedway race. Fewer than 20 of the event's 60 starters were still in contention when Johnson drove under the checkered flag some five-and-a-half hours after taking the starter's green.

Like many of the tracks of that time, Charlotte was underfinanced. Costs far exceeded projections and the facility had to be saved by reorganization under Chapter 10 of the Federal Bankruptcy Act. The revamping worked and the track, under

82

Aerial view of Charlotte Motor Speedway during the 1997 UAW-GM Quality 500.

ABOVE: Charlotte co-founder Bruton Smith.

LEFT: Shot of the condominiums overlooking turn No.1 at the Charlotte Motor Speedway.

83

area businessman Richard Howard, emerged as one of the most innovative and successful tracks on the circuit. Smith returned in the mid-1970s to reclaim ownership and begin a massive construction and improvement program that included building condominiums that overlook the track.

The track's events now include the Winston All-Star race held in May, the "600" the following week, and the UAW-GM 500, formerly the National 500 which began as the National 400, plus races for NASCAR's Busch Grand National Series, the Automobile Racing Club of America (ARCA), and the Indianapolis Racing League (IRL). In the early 1990s, the track erected lights so that it could present night events, and became the first big track to hold night events since the one-mile paved oval at Raleigh, N.C. did in the mid-1950s. The UAW-GM at Charlotte began in 1960 as a 400-mile event with Alfred "Speedy" Thompson driving a Wood brothers' Ford to the first victory. It was extended to its current 500 duration in 1965.

While Joe Lee Johnson was the first winner at the track, the list through 1997 has been extended to 33 names. Bobby Allison and

Darrell Waltrip head the track's "W" (winners) column with six each. Five of Waltrip's have come in the track's 600-mile event, an unprecedented number. Although the 600-mile Memorial Day weekend event still tests man and metal, three drivers have scored their initial career victories by winning it. David Pearson scored the first of his 105 career wins in the 1961 edition; Jeff Gordon won his first race in the 1994 running; and the following May, Bobby Labonte broke into the sport's winners' list with a breakthrough triumph. Matt Kenseth equalled their feat in the 2000 running.

Pole prowess on the track was exemplified by David Pearson who boasted 14 pole wins before retiring. From the fall of 1973 through the 1978 season, a string of 11 consecutive races, Pearson was the track's only pole winner. It is a streak unprecedented in the sport.

Charlotte's track and turns are still the same as initially designed, but the speeds have jumped since its beginnings. Roberts' pole-winning effort of 1960 seems slow when compared to the record 186.034 mph recorded by Dale Earnhardt, Jr., in the 2000 fall time trials. Robert's speed was turned 14 years before Dale Earnhardt, Jr., was born.

ABOVE: The sleek entranceway of the ultra-modern Charlotte Motor Speedway.

TOP: Cars coming off the 24-degree banking of turn No. 2, 1975.

BOTTOM: Charlotte was the first super-speedway to install lights for night racing, which cost them $1.7 million. The first nighttime Winston Cup race held there was on May 16, 1992. Here is a shot of a the now-obsolete Sportsman Division during a practice session under the lights.

Drivers get the green flag at Atlanta Motor Speedway to start the NAPA 500, the first NASCAR race run on the newly configured track, November 16, 1997.

Atlanta Motor Speedway

HAMPTON, GEORGIA

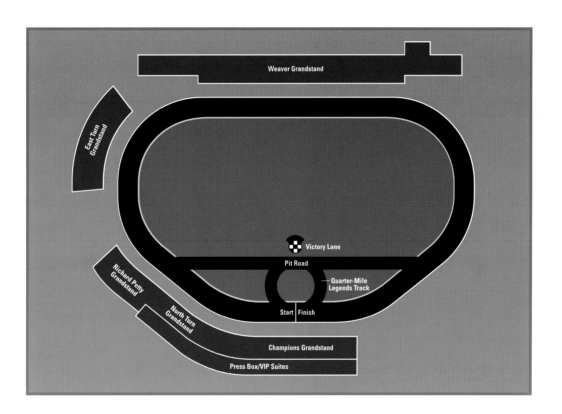

When it opened in July 1960, this facility, located some 25 miles south of downtown Atlanta, was the fifth of today's big tracks to present events for NASCAR's big league. Originally called "Atlanta International Raceway," it was the largest—and fastest—true oval on the circuit. The sweeping turns were banked at 24 degrees and the 180-degree direction changes cover a half mile at each end of the mile-and-a-half facility. The turns were connected by two equal quarter-mile straights.

Unlike the egg-shaped track at Darlington, S.C., the D-shaped Daytona Speedway, or the truncated tri-oval at Charlotte, the Atlanta track (actually located in the small community of Hampton, Ga.) was built with both sides equal. The exit of turn two was the same as its counterpart in turn four and the entries to turns one and three were also the same.

The track's inaugural event, the "Dixie 300" on July 31, 1960, found the legendary Fireball Roberts as the first pole winner. He pushed his black and gold Pontiac to 133.129 mph. Roberts went on to becomethe track's initial race winner as he led the 45-car field to the checkered flag.

In October of that year, the track hosted its second event, the season-ending "Atlanta 500," which again found Roberts atop the time-trial list, but saw Miami native Bobby Johns the honoree for the post-race celebration in the victory lane.

During the second season of its operation in 1961, the track elected to flip-flop the two races. The "Dixie," lengthened to a 400-mile distance, became the second race, although still run in mid-summer. The "Atlanta 500" became the track's opening event. It still runs in early March.

The track struggled with underfinancing and made it through a Chapter 11 bankruptcy reorganization before being bought by Bruton Smith in 1990 as part of his Speedway Motorsports group, which also includes the Charlotte, Bristol, and Texas tracks. Smith changed the facility's name to Atlanta Motor Speedway. Between the two events in 1997, the track was altered to mirror the Charlotte layout with two short dogleg turns connecting a brief straightaway the start-finish line sits. The change included a switch of the start-finish line from what had been the frontstretch to the back, thus making what had been turn one into turn three, although the bankings stayed the same.

The course's changes, plus new asphalt, increased the track's speed capability. The top time trial run in March 1997 was 186.507 mph, as posted by Chevy-driving Robby

Handling is paramount, as two-thirds of every lap is spent in the sweeping turns—even with the track's new design. A strong engine is a must here at the fastest track where carburetor plates aren't required.

Gordon in his first career pole win. On the new track that same November, Geoff Bodine blistered by the field at 197.478 mph in his Ford. Between Roberts' 1960 run and Bodine's '97 lap, some 34 drivers have won poles at Atlanta. Heading that list are Buddy Baker's seven, Cale Yarborough's half dozen, and five by Roberts before he was fatally burned in a wreck at Charlotte in 1964. During the same 37-year period, some 33 different drivers have earned race victories at Atlanta, most notably, Dale Earnhardt, with eight triumphs to his credit. Included among those is his victory in the 1980 Atlanta 500, the first big-track win of his career.

After Roberts' win from the pole position in 1960, no driver would win the "Dixie" race—which was extended to 500 miles in 1967—from the pole again for 27 seasons. Local favorite Bill Elliott ended that jinx as he took pole honors and went on to win the race in 1987 for one of the five victories for the red-headed driver from Dawsonville, Ga. Through the 1997 season Elliott was tied with retired Bobby Allison for fourth on the track's winner's list. They rank behind Earnhardt, Yarborough, and Richard Petty—who won there six times, before running his career final event on the track in 1994.

Drivers leaving the pits during the NAPA 500 at Atlanta, 1996.

88

ABOVE: Racing action
during Atlanta's inaugural
race, the Dixie 300,
July 31, 1960.

LEFT: Fireball Roberts, winner
of first two events at Atlanta
held in 1960: the Dixie 300
and the NAPA 500.

Dale Earnhardt
receives his trophy
at the NAPA 500,
1986.

The start of
the NAPA 500,
November 10, 1996,
the year before the
start-finish line was
moved to the
opposite side of
the track.

The 1998 Food City 500 takes place before the newly expanded facility, which nearly doubled its previous seating capacity of 70,000.

FOOD CITY

BRISTOL MOTOR SPE

Bristol Motor Speedway

BRISTOL, TENNESSEE

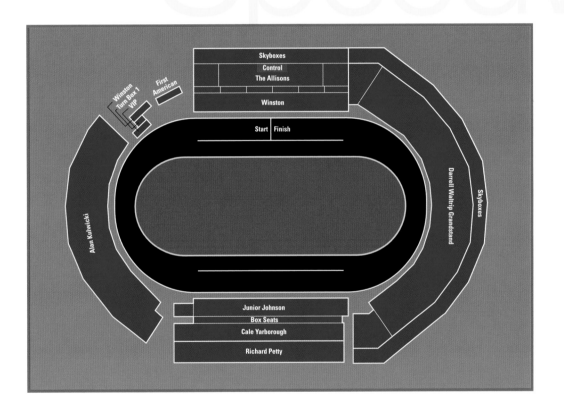

Although it's the second shortest track on the schedule, the .533-mile Bristol Motor Speedway located near the Tennessee-Virginia border, can proudly boast that it has the most steeply banked turns on the NASCAR circuit. At a slope of 36 degrees, the track's bowl-shaped layout features corners that are 5 degrees steeper than those at Daytona and 3 degrees more than Talladega—the biggest of the NASCAR tracks. Even Bristol's 650-foot long straights, at 16 degrees, are steeper than the turns at tracks in Phoenix, Martinsville, or Indianapolis.

But this wasn't always the case at Bristol. When it opened in 1961 the corners were banked at a mere 22 degrees. Ford's Fred Lorenzen was the old track's first pole winner with a pace of 70.225 mph. Spring of 1969, the last race held on the original track, found Dodge's Bobby Isaac on the pole with a speed of 88.669. Between the two 1969 races held there, the track was rebuilt to its present configuration and banking degrees. When the teams returned that summer, Cale Yarborough had to turn a lap of 103.432 in the Wood brothers' Ford to top the qualifying runs. Since Yarborough's first pole there on the rebuilt track, he outqualified the competition and set nine track record times before retiring in 1988. He earned three more pole positions

---

Size: 0.533 miles • Turn Banking: 36 degrees • Straight Banking: 16 degrees

than Richard Petty, who hung up his helmet with six No. 1 starts at the track. Mark Martin and Petty were tied through 1997 with six each. Martin took both Bristol poles in 1995 and 1996 for a string of four, a feat unprecedented in track history. Included was his record run in the summer of '95 when he turned a lap of 125.093.

Changed too, since its opening, is the facility's name. It was originally known as "Bristol International Speedway." It later became "Bristol International Raceway" before changing again, when purchased by Speedway Motorsports in mid-1996, to its present incarnation: Bristol Motor Speedway. Even the track's surface has changed over the years. Asphalt from inception through the spring race in 1992, the blacktop was torn out after that event and replaced with concrete.

Georgia's Jack Smith came from 12th in the starting lineup to become the track's inaugural winner and start its victory list—a column currently headed by Darrell Waltrip with a dozen triumphs. Included on Waltrip's list are seven straight wins while driving Junior Johnson's entries. (The seven consecutive wins equals the all-time record set by Richard Petty at Richmond between 1970 and 1975 for the most consecutive wins at any of the circuit's tracks.) The last Bristol victor before Waltrip began his string of wins was Yarborough, who also did it in a Johnson entry. Thus Johnson, a winner here himself as a driver in 1965, has the distinction as owner of eight straight winners at any track. The run by Waltrip and the respective wins by Yarborough

To succeed here on the steepest banked turns in the sport, cars need strong but responsive right-side suspension. Quick acceleration is a must on the short straightaways to make up speed lost in the corners.

TRACK TACTICS

and Johnson are some of the 21 triumphs enjoyed by team owner Johnson. Among active owners the nearest challenger is Richard Childress with six Bristol victories through 1997.

Two of Johnson's wins were historic. The first came in the summer event of 1971 as Johnson was trying to get Chevrolet back to its winning ways of the early 1960s. Charlie Glotzbach was his driver. The Indiana native had qualified second but proved to be the car to beat. The oppressive summer heat of that July afternoon was also unbeatable. Midway through the grueling 500 laps, Glotzbach waned. Johnson tapped Tennessee's Raymond "Friday" Hassler to be the relief driver. Hassler drove the car, despite time lost on the driver change, to a three-lap victory margin in the only caution-free event in track history at a record 101-plus mph.

Johnson's other unique Bristol triumph came in the spring race two years later, in 1973. This time, with Cale Yarborough driving, they won the pole and sprang to a healthy lead before unrelenting spring rains forced a halt after 52 laps had been run. Yarborough led them all. The rains didn't stop and the remainder of the race was rescheduled. When the race resumed two weeks later, Yarborough picked up where he left off, leading all of the remaining laps. The car held its lead throughout the delay and that event still marks the only time a driver has led for an entire 500-lap race. (During the postponement, Yarborough also drove Johnson's car to a second place finish in a 500-mile event at Rockingham while, technically, still leading at Bristol.)

94

In its more modest incarnation, Bristol hosts the Winston Cup, July 24, 1966.

A long view of the grandstands as the drivers get ready.

North Carolina Speedway

ROCKINGHAM, NORTH CAROLINA

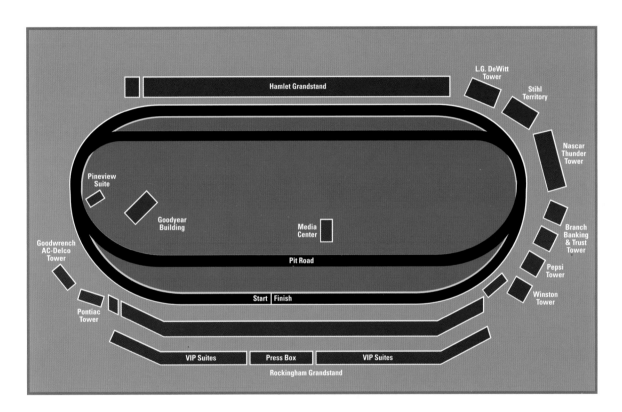

When it opened in the fall of 1965 as the "North Carolina Motor Speedway," it was the fifth of today's one-mile (or more) tracks. It joined the Darlington track, which had pioneered the group in 1950, the huge Daytona tri-oval's 1959 premier, and the mile-and-a-half Charlotte and Atlanta tracks, which had both come on board in 1960. Another four seasons would pass before another new track joined the circuit.

With low banking and measured an even mile in length, the oval had a bowed frontstretch to form a D-shaped oval, though not as harsh a bend as seen at Daytona, the only track with a similar configuration at the time. It did emulate both the Daytona and Darlington facilities by presenting a 500-mile race as its first event.

The field for that inaugural event was a cross-section of new and old drivers. Pioneers Ned Jarrett, Curtis Turner, Junior Johnson, and Buck Baker were still driving, but the sport's new talent was also emerging to supplant them in NASCAR's star galaxy. Buddy Baker was in the field with his dad; Richard Petty, a prince of his sport on his way to being crowned "The King"; and Cale Yarborough had already beaten the older stars, as had David Pearson. But the scenario was even more complex than that.

Size: 1.017 miles • Turn 1-2 Banking: 22 degrees • Turn 3-4 Banking: 25 degrees * Straight Banking: 8 degrees

In a rules dispute, the Chrysler racing division had boycotted the NASCAR season in 1965. As an appeasement to fans, the sanctioning body had lifted the ban imposed on Curtis Turner for trying to unionize the drivers. (Turner had been suspended a few years earlier when he attempted to organize the drivers so he could secure a loan from the Teamsters to salvage the troubled Charlotte track he'd founded.) The Chrysler camp had selected the Rockingham race, 54th and next to last race of the year, to return to their factory-backed Dodges and Plymouths.

Richard Petty put his Plymouth on the pole with a run of 116.260 mph, narrowly beating out Junior Johnson's Ford. Turner, in a second Wood brothers' Ford as teammate to Marvin Panch, started fourth alongside David Pearson in a

TRACK TACTICS

A good qualifying run gets you a front stretch pit, a must for winning. Suspension set-up is vital in the race where chassis can compensate for weaker power plant.

factory-back Cotton Owens' Dodge.

With two from each manufacturer—Ford and Chrysler—in the first two rows, the battle for supremacy continued when the green flag fell on the last day of October. Johnson pushed his mount around Petty in the first lap to become the first lap leader on the track. It would be a position he held for the first 45 circuits before Turner showed his layoff hadn't hampered his ability. Four more drivers worked their way to the front before the afternoon was over. It wasn't an easy battle for many. Tires blew, engines failed, spins and crashes were frequent. The final 100 miles found only Turner and Yarborough, driving Banjo Matthews' Ford, on the lead lap. Yarborough was ahead with 30 laps to go when he had to make his final pit stop. While he was being serviced, Turner drove by to take the lead he would

98

LEFT: Brothers Dan, Bill, and Ernie Elliott celebrate together in Victory Lane at North Carolina, October 1984.

RIGHT: Racing action during the Goodwrench Service 400, 1996.

not relinquish, thereby becoming the track's initial winner. It would be his 17th and final victory in a Hall of Fame career. (Turner died in a private plane crash five years later.)

Ford drivers swept the day. The highest non-Ford placer was Jim Paschal in fifth place in a team Plymouth from Petty's shops. The race took nearly five hours to complete (4 hours; 54 minutes). In the spring of 1966, the track added a second race to its schedule, also a 500-miler, and the Chrysler camp found redemption when Paul Goldsmith won from the pole driving a Nichels Engineering Plymouth. Finishing second, again, was Yarborough.

To enhance speeds, the track was redesigned by computer and the turns raised to their present bankings in 1969. It was the first track to be designed by a computer. Its new distance around was listed at 1.017 miles and a 500-mile race required 492 laps, eight laps fewer than before. The change worked—the pole speed jumped nearly 20 miles an hour. In 1997, the track shortened

both of its races to 400 miles, a distance that requires 393 laps.

On the old and new track the top winner has been Richard Petty. Before retiring at the end of the 1994 campaign, the original pole sitter had won there 11 times. He raced his only son, Kyle, there, and has seen him win three events that resulted in fatherly pride but a driver's disappointment. In all three victories Kyle beat, among others, his father.

In February of 1998, the track changed its name to North Carolina Speedway, although most fans and racers refer to it as "The Rock"—a track that's seen future stars first test themselves in racing's major league. Both Ricky Rudd (1975) and Bill Elliott (1976) both made their Winston Cup debuts in the track's events and both have won there. Kyle Petty and Hut Stricklin earned their first career poles on the track, and Mark Martin and Ward Burton scored their first career Winston Cup wins there to add their names to the winners' list begun there by Curtis Turner back in 1965.

ABOVE: Richard Petty receives the winner's trophy for the American 500, at the then-called
"North Carolina Motor Speedway," October 21, 1979.
RIGHT: Richard Petty leads into a turn during the ACDelco 400, November 1981.

The Miller 500 race begins at Dover, 1997.

Dover Downs International Speedway

DOVER, DELAWARE

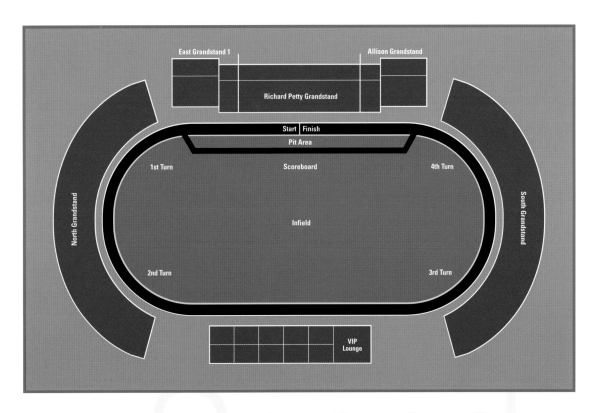

July 6, 1969 was significant in NASCAR's history. Prior to that date, the organization's major league had never demonstrated its intensity and skill in the state of Delaware. The division's events had been run in all of the states which abutted it and as far away as South Dakota and Oregon, but never had Delaware residents been able to see the races in person without leaving the "First State."

On the site of a former Delaware State Police barracks, a group of local businessmen had built a high banked one-mile oval that surrounded a trotting track for sulky racing. NASCAR officials had seen and approved the facility for its elite division. It was a true oval with equal-radius turns and parallel straights. Corners banked up at 24 degrees and even the straights were sloped at nine in the middle, and gradually tilted up to meet the incline of the turns. Dover entered its 30th anniversary year in 1999, as the largest and fastest true oval on the Winston Cup circuit, assuming the title when the Atlanta track was altered in 1997.

Driver David Pearson, at the controls of a blue and gold Holman-Moody Ford, was the track's 1969 inaugural race pole winner for the race that would be run just two days after the July Fourth event at Daytona. With a speed of 130.430 mph Pearson set the first standard for time trials there as he bettered

---

Size: 1.0 miles • Turn Banking: 24 degrees • Straight Banking: 9 degrees

a 32-car field's efforts. The first race on the track—and in the state—was scheduled for 300 miles. Just three factory supported cars entered: Pearson, LeeRoy Yarbrough in Junior Johnson's Ford, and Richard Petty who was also driving a Dearborn-backed Ford that season. They were also the only drivers to lead that day. Pearson led the first five laps contested. He was overtaken by Yarbrough who was passed by Petty. But attrition took its toll. First Pearson smacked the wall to end his hopes, then Yarbrough's white machine crashed. Their demise left Petty a clear shot home. He went on to a six-lap victory over Sonny Hutchins who was driving Junie Donlavey's Ford. It was one of the 10 victories claimed by Petty in 1969, the only season he drove Dearborn-made machines.

The following season, in 1970, the results were the same. Bobby Isaac in a Dodge was on the pole, but it was Petty and his crew celebrating in victory lane after another Dover win. The only difference in the second running was Petty's return to the Chrysler camp. He was in a Plymouth as he drove his second straight victory on the one-mile oval.

In its third year, and the track's spring race, then called the "Mason-Dixon," was extended to a full 500 miles, and had a new winner. Petty took pole honors for the event but Bobby

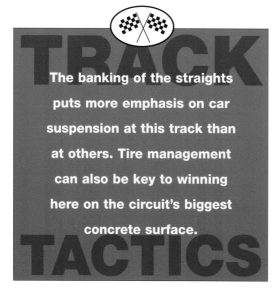

TRACK TACTICS

The banking of the straights puts more emphasis on car suspension at this track than at others. Tire management can also be key to winning here on the circuit's biggest concrete surface.

Allison, who succeeded Pearson in the Holman-Moody mount, won the track's first 500-mile race. In that 1971 season the track added a second 500-mile event—the "Delaware 500," which ended with Petty as its inaugural winner. The two races continued as 500s until the 1997 season when both were cut back to 400 laps, 400 miles, to shift their emphasis from endurance to competition.

The 12th year, 1981, with the track's spring race as a 500-miler, most obviously displayed the track's durability. David Pearson was again on the pole and was the event's first lap leader, but was later parked by a faulty engine. Neil Bonnett assumed command in the Wood brothers' Ford. He headed the field for 403 circuits, building a two-lap margin over Cale Yarborough's Buick, before engine maladies also put his machine in the garage. But it wasn't long before Bonnett was exiting the shower in the drivers' lounge when Yarborough entered, also the victim of his car's engine failure. Making up a five-circuit deficit, Jody Ridley took over the lead in Donlavey's Ford and went on to record his only victory in Winston Cup competition.

The track was changed from asphalt to concrete in the mid-'90s but remains as challenging to drivers and crews it was when it first brought the sport to Delaware in 1969.

TOP: Cars queued up during pre-race celebrations.

BOTTOM: A wide-angle shot of the first turn at Dover Downs, 1997.

Bird's eye view of the start-finish line and center grandstand at the start of the 1997 Miller 400.

Michigan Speedway

BROOKLYN, MICHIGAN

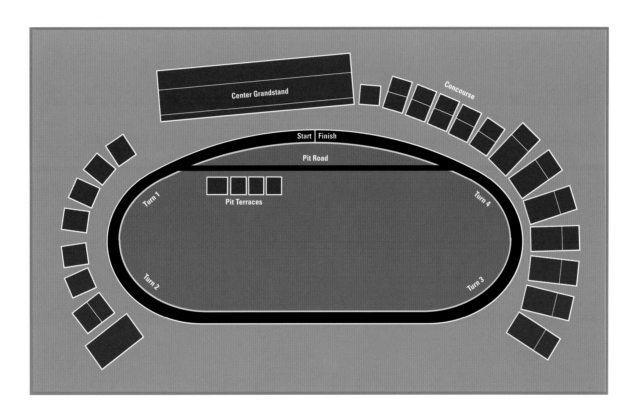

No season in Winston Cup history has seen its family of tracks expand as greatly as it did in 1969. That was the year that four new facilities, all super-speedways, entered the fold. Among these fledgling tracks was the Dover track in Delaware; the 2.66 mile ultra-fast track in Talladega; and the two-mile D-shaped inaugural at Texas World Speedway in College Station.

The first track to join the list of new Winston Cup venues that year was the modestly banked two-mile tri-oval in the Irish Hills resort area of Michigan. On June 15, 1969, the Michigan International Speedway (the "International" was dropped from the name in 1997) hosted its first Winston Cup event with the only 500-mile race ever contested there under the NASCAR banner.

The facility had been designed by Charles Moneypenny, a Floridian who'd also designed the Daytona track, created the one at Talladega, and would later design the remodeling of the track that now exists at Richmond, Va. Interestingly, when designing the Michigan track, Moneypenny relied on texts that were most commonly used to construct railroads and to compute the mathematics needed to create smooth grade change for trains. That formula seems to work perfectly for auto racing as well.

Size: 2.0 miles • Turn Banking: 18 degrees • Straight Banking: 12 degrees

Bumper-to-bumper racing action at Michigan Speedway.

When the stock car teams arrived at the track, which had hosted sports car events for its 1968 opening, they found smooth transitions (spirals) from the five-degree pitch of the back stretch to the 18-degree turns and from the fourth corner exit through the 12-degree slope of the tri-oval. They also found a wide racing surface that permitted two, three, even five abreast racing. Although the track was fast, they found the track's configuration to be conducive to intense, side-by-side competition as well.

Donnie Allison, in Banjo Matthews' poppy-red Ford, was the track's initial pole winner at 160.135 mph. He would not be, however, the first NASCAR driver to lead a race there. That honor went to LeeRoy Yarbrough who pushed Junior Johnson's Ford to the front in the initial lap. Allison did get back in front but was the fourth driver to do so among the nine who would lead the field during that afternoon.

Although the early laps were dramatic, the final one was what had the fans standing for a better view and talking for years to come. The final 30 laps of the race boiled down to a battle of the "Yarbs." LeeRoy Yarbrough and Cale Yarborough, with the latter piloting the Wood's red and white number "21" Mercury, swapped the lead five times in the last 60 miles. They took the white flag side by side and raced two abreast into the first turn and bumped. Yarbrough, on the high side, drifted up and hit the outer wall. Yarborough bobbled but regained control and went on to a five-second victory margin over David Pearson in the Holman-Moody Ford. LeeRoy's car ground along the wall for a mile and a half, sparks flying, and came to a halt just yards from the finish line, never finishing the last lap. His run, however, was good enough for fourth place in the track's initial NASCAR

TRACK TACTICS

Here speed and drafting play equal roles. Fuel consumption and tire wear require careful management. With its proximity to the car makers' offices, this track inspires extra team effort during races.

race. Later that summer the facility hosted its second event for NASCAR's major league, the "Yankee 600," thereby becoming only the second track, after Charlotte, to try a 600-mile race. Midwestern rains thwarted the attempt when the race had to be stopped after only 330 miles. Pearson, who'd earned the pole, was ahead when the skies opened. He was one of the dozen drivers that had led the race and among those who created the 26 changes of command seen in the total 165 laps that were run.

In 1970, the track shortened all of its events to 400 miles, 200 laps, the same distance that's run today. During subsequent seasons the speeds attained by NASCAR's finest increased some 30 mph above the initial pace, with Pearson its most frequent time-trial topper. He had 10 (four more than Bill Elliott) when he retired in 1986 from a 105-victory, 113-pole-winning career. Ten of his poles and nine race victories were recorded at Michigan. The numbers are the most by any drivers at the same track that's also seen as many as 63 start-finish line lead changes in a 200-lap race.

Situated just an hour west of the auto industry's home base in Detroit, the Michigan track is now owned by International Speedways and its events are watched closely and well attended by the car builders' engineers and executives who have helped swell the crowds to state records for sports events. That growth is also a tribute to the design ability of Charles Moneypenny.

In the summer of 1998 Jeff Gordon became the 20th driver to post a win on the track. At the same time he became the seventh driver to score four consecutive wins in Winston Cup racing during any season since 1972, when the schedule was reduced to approximately 30 events annually.

TOP: Driver Mark Martin claims the checkered flag in the Miller Lite 400, June 14, 1998, Michigan.

BOTTOM: Driver Richard Petty poses with his car in 1992 at the then-called "Michigan International Speedway."

Drivers racing through the tri-oval during the practice session,
October 11, 1997, for the following day's DieHard 500.

Talladega Superspeedway

TALLADEGA, ALABAMA

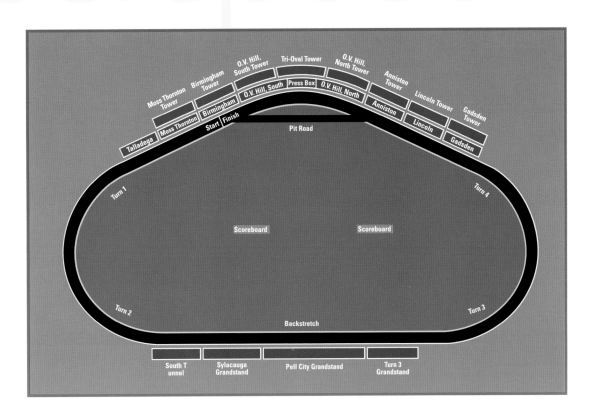

With its 1969 opening, the Talladega track immediately became the biggest and fastest oval in NASCAR's racing facilities. Longer and faster than Daytona, with the steepest and widest bankings of any of the circuit's big tracks, the place was designed for fast and close competition. Bill France Sr. got what he wanted—maybe more—when he asked Charlie Moneypenny to design it. The Florida engineer who had also designed the facility's sister track in Daytona as well as the then-new Michigan oval (and would later create the design for Richmond) gave him a track where speeds approached the 200-mph mark, yet one where cars could battle side by side.

Nearly 10 mph faster than Daytona and nearly 30 mph above that year's 170-mph pole speed for the Indy 500 (as recorded by A. J. Foyt), the drivers balked. The tire companies, who hadn't tested their wares at that speed, were suddenly faced with blistering tires that failed in the practice sessions. Many of the factory backed teams withdrew citing safety concerns. But France persevered. He enlisted cars and drivers from NASCAR's now defunct Grand Touring division, on hand to run a preliminary support race the day before the inaugural 500-mile event, to fill the field with their Camaros, Mustangs, and Cougars.

Size: 2.66 miles • Turn Banking: 33 degrees • Straight Banking: 2 degrees

Driving the orange K&K Insurance Company sponsored and owned Dodge Daytona prepared by master mechanic Harry Hyde, Bobby Isaac was the track's first pole winner with a lap speed of 196.386. His time was beaten in the next day's time trials by a purple Dodge Daytona piloted by "Chargin' Charlie" Glotzbach who circled the D-shaped oval at a breathtaking 199.466. Just 13 regular Winston Cup cars, many with substitute drivers including sophomore driver Richard Brickhouse (who replaced Glotzbach, who withdrew due to concern about tire durability) were on the line the morning of the race. The balance of the 36-car field was filled by the smaller Grand Touring machines. The race ran that September afternoon as scheduled. Seven drivers swapped the lead 35 times, many of those changes coming during the frequent pit stops that were required because of

> ### TRACK TACTICS
> Like Daytona, a strong engine and slick bodies are the "musts" on the circuit's biggest track. Here, drafting ability and calmness in heavy traffic are direct avenues to the winners' circle.

the tire problems. Brickhouse seized his opportunity by fronting the field six times and led the event's final 11 laps to take a seven-second victory over another winged, aerodynamic Dodge driven by Jim Vandiver. It would be the only major-league victory of Brickhouse's career.

The tire problem, which had led to the 1969 driver boycott was resolved before the circuit returned in 1970 and the track's promise of speed and competition became a reality. New England's Pete Hamilton drove a second Petty Engineering-owned Plymouth Superbird to victory in both Talladega races in 1970. Hamilton's summer victory at Talladega that year set the stage for what would be a string of different drivers winning the subsequent 13 Talladega races, representing a 12-year span. The string wasn't broken until Darrell Waltrip, who first won in

114

LEFT: Richard Brickhouse leads Jim Vandriver in the 1969 inaugural race at Talladega Superspeedway.

RIGHT: Richard Brickhouse in Victory Lane at Talladega, September 14, 1969, after winning the DieHard 500.

1979, won for a second time in 1982. The next season, 1983, found Dale Earnhardt, at that time another new face in Talladega's victory lane, who managed to repeat his performance in 1984 and become the first to win the race back-to-back. The track's second race, also a 500-mile, 188-lap test, won the first year by Hamilton, saw only three year's worth of first-time winners there before David Pearson who won it in '72, went on to win it again for the next two years straight.

With only 188 laps required to cover 500 miles, the Talladega races boast the fewest circuits run on any of the tracks that are a mile or more in length. Yet they have produced the three most competitive—four of the top five —races in the history of NASCAR's major league. 1984's spring race, won by Cale Yarborough, saw a NASCAR record: 75 official lead changes during the 188 laps. The summer race that same year had 68 exchanges of command before Earnhardt emerged the winner. The summer race of 1986 (it was moved to the fall in 1997) also marked a leader record. Of the 42 cars that started the chase, 26 had a turn at the front during the afternoon.

The all-time NASCAR qualifying record of 212.809 mph was set on the track in 1987's spring race by Bill Elliott, the red-headed Ford driver from Georgia. But an incident in that event led to a mandated slowing of the cars for races held there and at Daytona. Bobby Allison's engine failed in the track's 18-degree tri-oval less than 100 miles into the race. Pieces of metal cut the Buick's rear tires and sent the car spinning into the grandstand

fence, precariously close to the spectators at the start-finish line. After a lengthy delay for fencing repairs the race finished with, ironically, Allison's son, Davey, winning.

The incident alerted the NASCAR officials to potential spectator safety concerns and subsequently they imposed carburetor restrictor plates (which restrict the flow of fuel-air mixture to the cylinders, thereby slowing the car's speed capacity) on the engines of the cars for future races at the two tracks. The size of the restrictions have been periodically adjusted since, but the plates remain mandatory for those events and, fortunately, there's not be a recurrence of cars hurling into the fences. Later the roof flaps were required to prevent the cars from becoming airborne when the same aerodynamics that hold them down when running forward are reversed when a car turns sideways or backward at high speed.

Despite the slowing devices, the fastest race in NASCAR history was run with them in 1997. In the only caution-free event in this track's history, Mark Martin drove a Jack Roush-owned Ford to a winning 188.354 mph average for the 500 miles in the track's spring event. He beat Earnhardt to the line in that race by just 0.146 second. The track's second 500 in 1997 found Terry Labonte, despite four caution periods, winning by exactly the same margin over his younger brother Bobby, 0.146 second. It was the 22nd time in the division's history that brothers have finished first and second in placings in a Winston Cup race and the first time at Talladega since Donnie and Bobby Allison did it in the track's 1971 spring event.

116

ABOVE: Davey Allison poses with his trophy at the Winston 500, 1987.

A shot of the action at Talladega shows how wide the track is—easily allowing for four-abreast racing.

Drivers going into the
8-degree banking of turn
No. 2 at Pocono, 1996.

Pocono International Raceway

LONG POND, PENNSYLVANIA

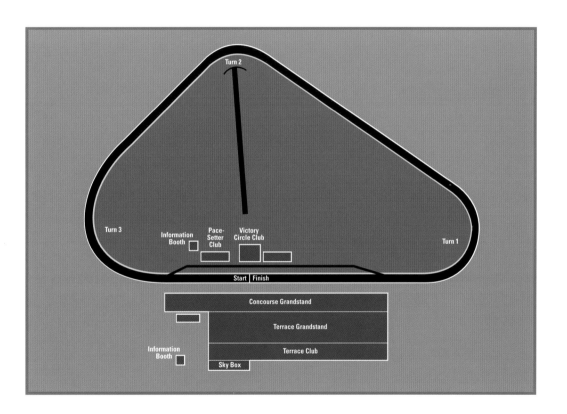

Many people assume NASCAR's Winston Cup circuit began as a southern sport. History shows that during its first season, 1949, two of the eight races were held in Pennsylvania. Another was held in New York state that year. In the late 1990s, 13 of 33 of the major league stock car races were held north of Virginia or west of the Mississippi River.

Although it was the 10th Pennsylvania facility to host the Cup series, Pocono International Raceway's inaugural race in 1974 ended a nine-year absence of the circuit in the Keystone State.

To some, this three-turn track looks like an oval designed by committee. Each corner has a different degree of banking and none of the three straightaways are the same length. The unusual configuration is a nightmare for the crews who have to set up the cars. If you set up the chassis for the 14-degree first turn, it will be "off" in the third turn's 6-degree banking. That's just one degree more than the bankings of straightaways at tracks like Daytona or Charlotte. Gearing the transmission and rear end combinations is no easier than setting the springs and shocks. The flat "north straight," which connects turns two and three, is just 1,780-feet long. If the gear ratios are set up properly for it, the engine will overwind on the 3,740-foot-long main straight between turns three and one. Likewise, the "long-pond straight," connecting turn one and two, is 3,055 feet long.

Although it's been a challenging track to both crews and drivers for more than two decades, drivers have met its challenge and provided some great competition. Those battles have included some five- to seven-car-wide battles for position down the long, broad homestraight before they funnel into the tightest turn of the three.

The track was built by the Mattioli family in 1970 and opened in 1971. During the first three years it hosted 500-mile Indy car races, United States Auto Club (USAC) stock car

TRACK TACTICS

Compromise of chassis is the trick to winning at this track. The unique tree turn design challenges every team's chassis set-up, and the differences in straightaway lengths defy the gear specialists. Engines and gearing are vulnerable here.

events and other races while awaiting a Winston Cup date. When the big league arrived in 1974, NASCAR's finest proved the wait worthwhile.

The first time trial session resulted in Buddy Baker taking the initial NASCAR pole on the 2.5-mile triangle at 144.122 mph in a Bud Moore-engineered Ford. Bobby Allison, in his own Chevrolet, earned the other front row berth for the inaugural event.

Baker led the first two laps contested that early August afternoon, only to have the first lead change occur in the third lap. Richard Petty shot by Baker's Ford to take command. Summer rains forced the inaugural event to be red flagged after 300 miles with Allison ahead. It took just over an hour for the

Drs. Joe and Rose Mattioli (CENTER AND RIGHT) cut the ribbon to inaugurate the 2.5-mile tri-oval Pocono International Raceway with William Smyth, 1971.

Steve Park's car is serviced at the Pocono International Raceway, 1997.

storm to pass and complete track drying, but the race did resume—to be stopped again by another storm eight laps short of the attempted 200 laps, or 500 miles. Petty's Dodge held almost a 19-second margin over Baker's Ford when the race was halted for the second and final time, making Petty the first Winston Cup winner at Pocono.

The track added a second 500-mile race to its schedule in 1982 with Cale Yarborough taking pole honors and Bobby Allison the winner of that event's first running.

In the second event there in 1979, Dale Earnhardt was injured in a wreck while leading as the race neared the halfway mark. Earnhardt missed starting the next few events and David Pearson was enlisted to replace him while he recuperated. Pearson won the Southern 500 in Earnhardt's car at Darlington. The following week, Earnhardt was back in the car at Richmond building a streak of more than 500 consecutive starts. His list of

consecutive starts is second only to Terry Labonte's, which passed the 500-point some 23 races before Earnhardt.

In the summer race of 1987, a terminally ill Tim Richmond scored his fourth Pocono victory and the next to last of his 13 career wins. Richmond died from the illness while he was tied (with Darrell Waltrip) as the winningest Cup driver at the track.

In the first lap of 1988's second Pocono event, Bobby Allison, who'd beat out his son in a one-two family finish in that year's Daytona 500, was involved in a second-turn wreck that nearly claimed his life. It did end his 84-win career and occured on the track where he'd won three 500- mile races in Cup competition.

The two races in the lush Pocono Mountain resort area track are held just six weeks apart—the shortest interval between races at any of the facilities that host two annual events for Winston Cup races.

122

LEFT: Driver Richard Petty celebrates in Victory Lane after the Acme 500, 1973.
RIGHT: Driver Darrell Waltrip celebrates with his wife, Stevie (LEFT), after winning the Mountain Dew 500 at Pocono, July 26, 1981.

A direct view of the start-finish line and the Victory Circle Club at Pocono from the grandstands.

Dale Jarrett tries to pass an out-of-control
Dale Earnhardt during the Dura-Lube 500
as he spins through turn No. 4 at Phoenix
International Raceway, November 2, 1997.
Jarrett won; Earnhardt placed 5th.

Phoenix International Raceway

PHOENIX, ARIZONA

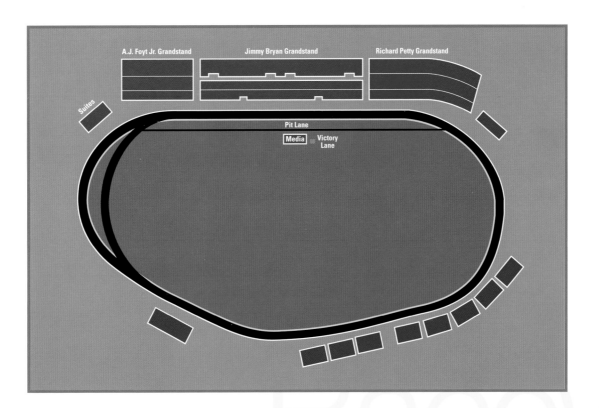

Arizona's capital city hosted NASCAR's major division in the 1950s when car-maker pioneers like Hudson's Marshall Teague, Buck Baker, and Tim Flock—the latter in Chrysler 300s—won events on the one-mile dirt track at the State Fairgrounds. But it wasn't until the closing of the road course at Riverside, Calif., in 1987, that the Winston Cup circuit moved permanently to the paved one-mile track a few miles west of Phoenix in Avondale, where it sits among the tall saguaro cactus and abutting Indian-owned land.

This track is uniquely shaped. From the air it looks D-shaped but, unlike similarly configured facilities, Phoenix has a straight homestretch and the bowed backstretch. Its arc leads toward the cactus-studded hillside, a popular viewing area for spectators.

The track, although demanding, was immediately popular with the race teams and spectators. The singular annual race there quickly became the largest and best-attended sporting event in the state. It has, in the first 10 seasons (through 1997), proven to be an elusive contest to win from the pole—a goal none had attained—and for repeat winners. Nine drivers won in the first 10 events there. Only the late Davey Allison was able to do it more than once. This second-generation Cup driver

---

Size: 1.0 mile • Turns 1-2 Banking: 11 degrees • Turns 3-4 Banking: 9 degrees

won the 1991 event there and returned the following year to score again.

In the years before Winston Cup races were held there, some of NASCAR's other divisions, such as the Winston West, had already raced on the track. Many of the senior division's drivers, such as Neil Bonnett, Cale Yarborough, and Richard Petty, who raced in those events, did well. Each emerged triumphant in Winston West events. When the Cup teams rolled onto the track in November 1988, the first pole was won by Geoff Bodine at 123.203 mph in a Rick Hendrick-owned Chevy. But the race had a surprise winner, Alan Kulwicki. Starting from 21st position on race day, Kulwicki was in his own Ford and still seeking a first career victory. In the waning laps it appeared his quest would not be realized as the Kenny Bernstein-owned Buick piloted by Ricky Rudd was stretching his lead over Kulwicki and the rest of the 43-car field. As the race, which is 500 kilometers (312 miles on a one mile track), neared the 300-lap point, the Buick's engine soured. Wisconsin's Kulwicki motored past the disappointed Rudd and led the final 16 revolutions.

The engineering graduate from the University of Wisconsin who'd chosen to race cars instead of design them; who'd moved to North Carolina's hub of the sport with no promise of success and built his own team from the ground up, had tears streaming as he got the checkered flag. While taking his cool-down lap, Kulwicki suddenly spun the car around as he passed the checkered flag a second time. He promptly

This track tests cars' brakes and suspensions. The unique backstretch "bow" makes the third turn entry the fastest spot on the track, where heavy braking helps turn the car.

took a reverse tour around the track in what he called his "Polish Victory Lap" to celebrate his long-sought triumph.

His victory in the Valley of the Sun was the first of five wins he would enjoy during a championship career cut short by a fatal airplane accident in 1993, on the way to a race at Bristol, Tenn.

In 1996, the track saw another first. Since retiring at the end of his 200-victory, seven-championship driving career at the end of the 1994 season, Richard Petty had remained active in Winston Cup competition as an owner. His new role had not found the success he'd known as a driver, at least not until his team got to Phoenix for the next-to-last race of the 1996 season. That was the event in which Bobby Hamilton, who'd begun his day from 17th position in the field, drove Petty's Pontiac to victory lane, giving "The King" his first victory as the owner of a car he wasn't also driving. It also extended a string of victories for the Petty family that began in the 1949 inaugural season of the division when Richard's father, Lee, had become the sixth man to win one of the division's races. Hamilton was the 149th, according to NASCAR's records.

In the 1997 edition of the race, Dale Jarrett won from ninth place on the starting grid and became one of only three drivers to win any of the track's initial 10 events from a top-10 starting position. No winner in those Phoenix races had begun his victory march from the front row until Jeff Burton started second and won in 2000.

ABOVE: Fans turn the cactus-studded hillside into a makeshift grandstand at Phoenix, 1997.

RIGHT: A 1996 aerial view of the Phoenix International Raceway.

126

Drivers navigate through the new turn called the Chute (which replaced turns No. 4, 5, and 6) during a practice lap for the SaveMart-Krager 350K, June 26, 1998.

Sears Point Raceway

SONOMA, CALIFORNIA

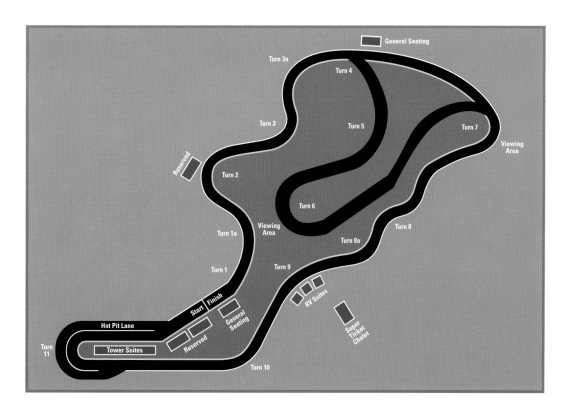

Among all forms of motorsports, none requires the diversity of abilities for driver and mechanic as NASCAR's elite Winston Cup. To make it to the highest level of stock car racing, drivers must be able to race on the greatest variety of tracks of any form of auto racing. They must successfully ply their craft on the big, fast tracks like Daytona and Talladega as well as on the short, tight circuits like Martinsville. The competitors must have the skills to battle side by side on intermediate-sized ovals like Charlotte and Michigan, as well as on the uniquely shaped layouts, such as Pocono and Darlington. They will also be called upon to stand up to the test of road racing: the braking, shifting, and turning—left as well as right—at top speed.

The road racing facet of the sport's major league dates from 1954, when NASCAR's new car division first tested itself on a two-mile twisting layout of the taxiways and runways of the Linden, N. J. airport. To attract sports car fans, NASCAR allowed European makes to enter against the big Detroit and Dearborn machines. Although Olds-driving Buck Baker took pole honors, the event was won by Al Keller in a Jaguar owned by famed orchestra leader Paul Whiteman. It marked the only event in Winston Cup history won by a foreign-manufactured car.

While the Linden race was the first time the big machines (NASCAR's Winston Cup cars are the largest and heaviest in any form of motorsports) challenged themselves on a road circuit, they had raced at eight other courses, including, among others, the 2.5-mile dirt circuit in Willow Springs, Calif.; the long 4.1-mile Elkhart Lake facility in Wisconsin; the Long Island's Bridge-hampton course; a nine-tenths-mile, now defunct, facility at the Bremerton, Wash. airport; the famed Watkins Glen track in New York; and southern California's Riverside Raceway, before competing at Sears Point in the Napa Valley wine country just north of the San Francisco Bay area.

Riverside ran its last race in mid-1988, with Ricky Rudd the final pole sitter and Rusty Wallace triumphant in the track's last event. With that track's closing, Sears Point, located 500 miles north of Riverside, moved onto the division's schedule and held its first event on the 2.52-mile layout complete with a dozen turns on June 11, 1989. Ironically, the same two drivers were successful, though in opposite places. Wallace, driving the Blue Max Pontiac, emerged as the track's first Winston Cup pole winner with a 90.041 mph lap. The checkered flag of the track's first Winston Cup race fell on Rudd, driving the green Kenny Bernstein-owned Buick, just 1.1 seconds ahead of Wallace after 187 miles of battling. Only 14 of the 42 starters were on the lead lap at the end.

The next year the Winston Cup cars and stars returned. While other drivers were now more familiar with the serpentine facility and its elevation changes, the same two drivers, Rudd and Wallace, made the headlines. Rudd was again on a road course pole (he'd take that honor for three of the first four races there) and Wallace the first to the finish line. Wallace would

As at all road courses, smooth equals fast. The gear train takes a beating as do the brake systems. A driver's ability to shift and brake smoothly while conserving tires is vital at this track

TRACK TACTICS

repeat his winning ways there in the tour's 1997 visit, also.

In 1991, Rudd, driving a Rick Hendrick-owned Chevrolet, nearly got his second Sears Point victory in the race. He and Davey Allison were vying for the lead in the horseshoe-shaped last turn, heading for the one-lap-to-go signal. Trying for a low-side pass, Rudd's orange Chevy popped the black right rear quarter panel of Allison's Ford. Allison spun, losing the lead. Rudd motored on to an apparent win. NASCAR ruled the contact excessive and penalized Rudd five seconds, making Allison the winner.

The track had proven a difficult place to display the frequent passing common in most stock car races—a significant factor in ensuring competition. The track was altered in 1998 to eliminate turns four, five, and six and make a straightaway, which runs downhill from the highest point of the track and connects again at the entry of what was the hairpin turn number seven. The change affords fans a better view of the track's action and affords the competitors more chances for lead swapping and battles for positions.

On the 12-turn configuration in 1995's event, Dale Earnhardt scored the first road race victory of his career. "The Intimidator" pushed his black machine around the twisting facility to take a victory over Mark Martin (who'd win there in 1997) to add a road circuit triumph to the list of short, inter-mediate, and super track victories in his seven-championship career. Although many don't usually consider him a threat on road courses, Earnhardt had won poles at Riverside, Watkins Glen, and at Sears Point before visiting any of their victory lanes. In fact, the first pole of his Cup career came at the Riverside track during his 1979 rookie season.

130

A view of Jeff Gordon's car in turn No. 2 at Sears Point's serpentine road course during the SaveMart-Krager 350K, June 28, 1998.

Driver Jeff Gordon celebrates his
Brickyard 400 win, August 1, 1998.

Indianapolis Motor Speedway

INDIANAPOLIS, INDIANA

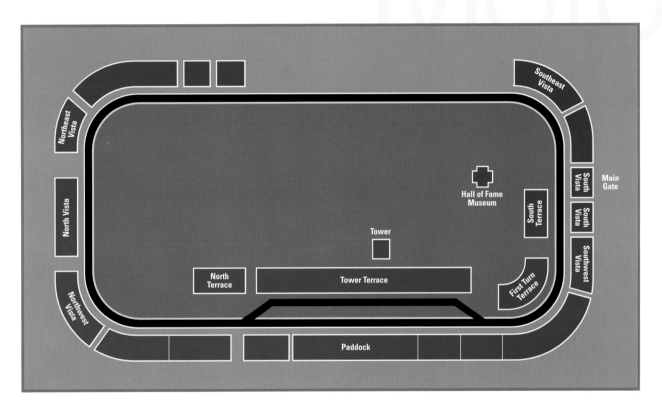

No first-time NASCAR event at any track has had the impact that the hallowed home of the Indianapolis 500 had when it hosted Winston Cup racing for the first time in 1994. It was immediately the richest event ever held in the history of the sanctioning body. It also attracted the biggest crowd of spectators to ever watch the big league perform.

From the opening laps of practice through the final lap of the inaugural "Brickyard 400," die-hard stock car fans were joined by their Indy car counterparts—some of whom were skeptical and even resentful of what they termed "NASCAR taxi cabs" stealing their thunder as they roared across the bricks at the start-finish line. But many were also impressed as the 3,500-pound machines negotiated the four, low-banked corners, hugged the quarter-mile short chutes, and flew down the 5/8-mile twin straights two, three, and four abreast. As the huge crowd left the track that August afternoon, virtually all knew they had seen more than just a stock car racing event. They had been part of a "happening."

Rick Mast gave himself a place in history by being the first stock car pole winner at the track, which had featured only the open-wheeled Indy cars since racing began there in 1911. The Virginia driver's 172.414 mph time trial effort, albeit slower

Cars approach turn No. 1 on the last pace lap before the start of the Brickyard 400, August 2, 1997.

than the speeds of May's "500," enshrined him as the first top NASCAR qualifier at Indy. He beat out Dale Earnhardt by two-tenths of a second for the honor and topped a 43-car field of starters. Joe Ruttman, younger brother of 1952 Indy 500 winner Troy Ruttman, was the fastest of the cars that failed to qualify. He missed the chance to compete, on the track where his brother had raced, by a mere two-thousandths of a second.

At a site where names like Foyt, Andretti, Unser, and Vuckovich were spoken, the public address speakers now blared names like Earnhardt, Jarrett, Petty, Wallace, Elliott, and Bodine. The scream of turbo-charged power plants was replaced by the chest-vibrating guttural roar of V-8s. Though the atmosphere was different, the purpose was the same: Every entrant was striving to complete the given distance in the least possible time. It is the goal in May and now the intent in August, as well.

Race they did in August. Mast led the first two laps before local hero Jeff Gordon took over to create the first NASCAR lead change. Before the affair was over, some 13 of the 43 starters had taken turns leading, a position they swapped among them 21 times during the 160 laps. Among those who lead were all three of the Bodine brothers—Geoff, Brett, and Todd, in their first appearance at the rectangular track. It marked the first time

> ### TRACK TACTICS
> The four-cornered design tests brakes twice as much as on an oval and the short chute gearing isn't right for the longer straights. Suspensions must be tuned to the track or the car bogs down in the turns.

three siblings from a family had ever led a race at the track.

The final five lead changes were between familiar Indianapolis names, Andretti and Gordon. But this time its was John Andretti, nephew of the 1969 Indy 500 winner Mario, and Jeff Gordon, rather than Gordon Johncock, the 1973 winner who repeated his victory in 1983. With just five laps to go, Gordon nosed his Chevy around Andretti's machine and went on to take a half-second victory. His efforts earned him a NASCAR record $613,000 for the weekend's efforts—marking the richest single event payoff in stock car history at the time. The youthful Gordon had moved to Indiana years before and developed his driving skills in midgets and sprint cars before moving up to NASCAR competition.

Since that inaugural event, Dale Earnhardt, Dale Jarrett, Ricky Rudd, and Bobby Labonte added their names to the unique trophy presented the winners. In 2001 Gordon became the first driver to win the 400 a third time. Spectators have packed the grandstands to watch every one of the subsequent editions of the 400-mile chase. Many who were skeptical at the first one have become ardent fans of the event they felt might diminish the Indy 500. Those feelings proved unfounded as the NASCAR competitors have presented a performance each year which has only enhanced the renown of racing at the "Brickyard."

Driver Ricky Rudd kisses the yard of bricks at Indianapolis after winning the Brickyard 400, August 2, 1997.

136

Fans celebrate the Brickyard 400 Inaugural Race, which was won by Jeff Gordon, 1994.

Drivers take turn No. 3 during the Jiffy Lube 300 at the New Hampshire International Speedway, July 1998.

New Hampshire International Speedway

LOUDON, NEW HAMPSHIRE

Two significant moments occurred on July 12, 1993. The first was the arrival of NASCAR's Winston Cup racing in New Hampshire, one of the few states in the eastern half of the country that had never hosted NASCAR's major league—and breaking a 23-year racing drought for the circuit in New England. Second, it marked the first time the circuit had raced on a track built primarily to host the WC series, as opposed to the minor leagues, and the first time they'd raced on a brand new site since the late 1960s when Talladega, Dover, Michigan, and the now-defunct Texas World Speedway had come on board.

Although it's true that during the same 23-year drought the Winston Cup teams had raced at facilities that were new to them. Places like Phoenix, Watkins Glen, and Sears Point were in operation long before the Cup teams' initial arrival. Richmond had also remodeled and rebuilt its track but remained on the site and in the state where they raced since the 1950s. But New Hampshire's new 1.058 mile, low-banked oval, which arose on the site of a former motorcycle road circuit, was wholly new to the thundering elite league. Its creation afforded the teams and their sponsors the opportunity to perform before an audience that was entirely new to the sport and the series, in addition to their loyal fans from the rest of the New England area. Further, it was the northern most site for the circuit since they'd raced in Maine during the mid-1960s.

Construction on the New Hampshire track had begun in 1989 and the initial NASCAR event there was a Busch Grand National Series race the following season. The track's low banking and tight-radius corners proved difficult for the drivers.

The track has a policy of tidying up its facility after each day's activity, including painting over any marks on the retaining wall from car contact. After the initial day of practice for the Busch division campaigners, the touching up required 33 gallons of paint. It's sufficient to say the track is demanding, even for the division considered to have second best driving talents among the sanctioning body's array.

After three years of presenting events for other divisions of NASCAR competition, the track was granted a Winston Cup date in 1993. The retaining wall required less post-practice repainting, but even the top drivers found the track's low bankings seriously challenging. The division's inaugural time trials found Mark Martin, in a Jack Roush-owned Ford, topping the list with a lap of 126.871 mph—produced in unseasonably hot—nearly 100-degree—weather. (Most had expected cooler New England climate after the previous week in Florida's tropical conditions at Daytona.) The field saw two Busch drivers making their initial start in the race. Both Joe Nemechek and Jeff Burton, opting to utilize their prior experience on the track from Busch events in making their first try at the sport's highest level, earned a starting spot. (Three years later, Burton would return to win the race.)

Martin would earn the distinction of being the first driver to lead a Cup race on the New Hampshire track. The Arkansas native was the first of six drivers who led the inaugural event during the 300 laps of competition. The biggest lap leader of the day was Sterling Marlin in the Stavola brothers' Ford who commanded the race three times for 123 laps before encountering late problems and finishing sixth. Rusty Wallace, in Roger Penske's Pontiac, had qualified 33rd in the 40-car field,

A view of cars navigating through turns No. 1 and 2 from the Concord Grandstands at New Hampshire.

but had worked his way into the lead pack as the laps waned. He was nearly six seconds behind leader Davey Allison when the sixth and final caution flag appeared. Wallace's crew made a speedy service stop to put him ahead of the field and he went on to become the track's first Winston Cup winner. He was 1.3 seconds ahead of Martin when he passed the checkered flag. Allison finished third in what proved to be his final race. The following week he was fatally injured in a heli-copter crash at the Talladega track in his native Alabama.

In the fall of 1997, the track was granted a second Winston Cup race and replaced the pioneer short-track facility at North Wilkesboro, N.C., on the schedule. It was held Sept. 14 with Ken Schrader taking pole honors and Jeff Gordon that event's first winner. Both were repeat performances at the track.

TRACK TACTICS

This track's low banking puts the premium on tires and suspensions. The flat corners scuff off speed, so proper gear selection is necessary to get it back quickly on the straights. Tire management is essential.

Schrader, a veteran of sprint car and midget racing before moving to the top of NASCAR's divisions in the mid-'80s, was the pole winner at the New Hampshire layout for that season's July stop. Gordon, another veteran of open wheel and cockpit circuits before becoming a Winston Cup champion, had won the track's singular 1995 event after starting 21st.

This modern facility was nearly forced to scrap the planned upper levels of its highrise grandstands—and the corporate suites that top them—because local authori-ties didn't own fire equipment that could reach the upper areas. The problem was resolved and the structure finished as planned when the Bahre family, who built and own the track, purchased and then donated an ample fire and ladder truck to afford access.

Mark Martin (RIGHT) passes Jeff Gordon for second place during the Jiffy 300, July 12, 1998.

The #33 car in the pits during the Slick 50 300 at New Hampshire International Speedway, July 1993.

Mark Martin celebrating his Texas 500 victory
at the Texas Motor Speedway, April 5, 1998.

Texas Motor Speedway

FORT WORTH, TEXAS

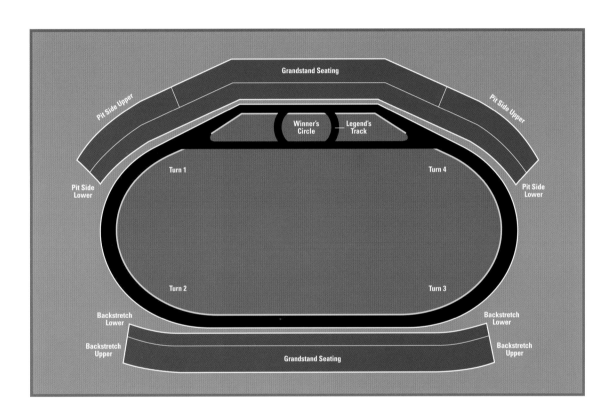

Although big, the state of Texas had been the site of only two tracks that have hosted Winston Cup events before the 1997 opening of this 1.5-mile facility modeled after its sister track, Charlotte Motor Speedway, in North Carolina. Both had a common founder, Bruton Smith, and each was built with a double dogleg frontstretch. They both afforded the race teams big 24-degree banked turns and a main (grandstand) gap from turn four to turn one consisting of two short chutes that connected on either side of the start-finish line straightaway.

But the similarities between the Tarheel facility and the Lone Star state's track ended there. Many teams assumed that the Charlotte chassis set up and gearing would work at the new track. They would learn it was not to be.

The radius of the Texas turns was longer than those at its eastern counterpart. Hence the machines carried more speed through the corners (not as much speed was "scrubbed off" by the friction of the Texas corners as in the tighter radius of the Charlotte track). Also the short chutes were not as long in Texas as the North Carolina track's. It quickly became obvious the Texas track was a whole new animal—for sure, a very different track.

In 1969 the NASCAR major league made its first venture

to the state, coming to race at the new two-mile, 22-degree tri-oval of Texas World Speedway near Texas A&M University at Bryan-College Station. Plagued by inclement weather, the track, which was commonly owned by the Michigan Speedway founders, hosted the final event of the 1969 campaign with Bobby Isaac as the inaugural Winston Cup winner in Texas. Just eight races were run there before the last event was held in 1981. Benny Parsons was the final winner. (Parsons also won the ninth and last Winston Cup race at California's Ontario Motor Speedway the previous season.)

The only other facility in the state to present Texans with NASCAR's motor sports major league was the half-mile Joseph Meyer Speedway oval in Houston. Bobby Allison won a 300 lapper in June 1971, the only Cup race ever run there.

Preparing for the first race at the new track was further complicated by the nemesis of the state's other big track—rain.

Three days of it negated much of the scheduled practice and swamped the spectator parking areas. Time trials were canceled in order for the teams to get some valuable practice laps and prepare their machines for the race. Dale Jarrett, driving Robert Yates' Ford, was appointed to the pole as the driver of the car leading in the Series' car owner point standings. The rest of the top 35 spots were similarly aligned by owners' points. The balance of the field was positioned by virtue of rule book procedures: former series champion; race winner of the season or previous year; finally by postmark dates on other entries as received at NASCAR headquarters in Florida. Thus Jarrett was the inaugural event's pole starter but the track entered its second season without a pole winner from time trials. It was a unique situation

TRACK TACTICS

This track may look like Charlotte, but doesn't act like it. Longer radius turns and shorter straights require different chassis set-ups and other gear ratios. Longer turns are harder on the tires as well.

not found at the opening of another of the circuit's facilities.

If track officials thought getting the field arranged was a problem, the opening lap of the inaugural event was a disaster. As the field entered the first turn for the first lap some 13 of the 43 starters were involved in a wreck. Just three-time Cup champion Darrell Waltrip, the only winner of a Texas Winston Cup race (1979) in the field, was eliminated by the mishap but several other potential contenders lost valuable time and laps while repairs were made. All were eliminated from the list of potential winners. Even so, some 10 drivers exchanged the lead during the 334-laps which comprised the 500 miles at the track. Another big wreck, this one involving just nine cars, further reduced the field at the event's halfway mark.

The Rouch racing team had problems. Mark Martin and Ted Musgrave both went to the garage prematurely with engine problems. But the the third teammate, Jeff Burton, soldiered on. He led the event twice for 60 laps but 58 of those were the event's final circuits. The young Virginian became the first Winston Cup winner at the track and did so with his first career victory. Burton crossed the finish line just four seconds ahead of fellow Ford driver Dale Jarrett.

The victory made Burton the 149th driver to win a Winston Cup race since the division's founding in 1949. It also made him the fourth driver to score their first big time triumph in a track's initial event. By claiming the Texas triumph he joined Johnny Mantz who did it in the first ever Darlington race, Richard Brickhouse the inaugural winner at Talladega and Alan Kulwicki the driver who won the first of the Phoenix races for his initial career triumph.

146

View of pit lane and the start-finish line at the 2.0-mile California Speedway during the inaugural California 500, June 22, 1997, the first year the track opened.

California Speedway

LOS ANGELES, CALIFORNIA

The two-mile, tri-oval facility in southern California's Los Angeles area was the newest facility when it joined the circuit in 1997. It extended, however, a long affiliation with the area dating back nearly 40 years. During that period many races were run in the southern half of the state. The two most notable facilities were the road course at Riverside, where NASCAR's major league raced from 1958 until its closing in 1988, and the now-defunct Ontario Motor Speedway (which sat just a few miles west of this track) that hosted the circuit between 1971 and 1980.

Series and team sponsors, as well as race fans, had requested a return of the sport to the densely populated and media-rich area. Their hopes were answered when Roger Penske, already the owner of the Michigan and Nazareth Speedways, announced his plans to erect a new track on an abandoned industrial site. With input from NASCAR officials, the site was granted a Winston Cup date even before it was constructed. It was an unprecedented move. Many tracks are built and conduct smaller events for a couple of years before they they are considered for a Winston Cup race.

The track copied the successful design of Michigan Speedway. A two-mile, D-shaped tri-oval with an arched frontstretch and a track width that accommodates four and five abreast racing. But the California track's design deviated from its Midwestern sister when the corner banking was lowered from Michigan's 18 degrees to 14 degrees for the Western layout.

The lower bankings did not alter the speed differential between the two similarly shaped tracks very much. In mid-June 1997 at Michigan, Dale Jarrett put a Robert Yates' Ford on the pole with a lap of 183.669 mph. The next weekend at the new West Coast facility, Joe Nemechek drove a Felix Sabates-owned Chevrolet to his first career pole winning lap of 183.015.

The California Speedway's inaugural race by the NASCAR stars also proved the wisdom of its design. Of the 42 starters, a dozen were able to lead the race. The command swapped hands 21 times with Jeff Gordon, a Californian by birth, going on to lead the final circuits and then becoming the first winner.

TRACK TACTICS

Wonderfully designed for racing, this track is similar to Michigan but with flatter corners, which puts more emphasis on suspension and tires. Fuel conservation is also a key at the circuit's most western track.

It marked the second inaugural victory of Gordon's career, which also included a triumph in the 1994 inaugural stock car race at Indianapolis Motor Speedway in, ironically, the driver's adopted state of Indiana.

In its opening event, Nemechek joined Curtis Turner at Darlington and Bob Welborn at Daytona as a track's inaugural pole winner. Gordon positions his name alongside Lee Petty at Daytona, Johnny Mantz at Darlington, and Fireball Roberts at Atlanta as the first winner of inaugural events at one of the sport's major venues.

Both the Riverside and Ontario tracks of the area have fallen prey to urbanization. The new California Speedway, which also hosts Indianapolis-type races and other NASCAR divisions, has risen on reclaimed land and returned the major leagues of motorsports to race fans of southern California.

150

Motor home campers watch the race from California Speedway's reserved infield section.

The inaugural California 500 begins at the California Speedway before a crowd of 80,000, June 22, 1997.

Drivers getting in the groove at the Las Vegas
400, the inaugural Winston Cup race, Las Vegas
Motor Speedway, March 1, 1998.

Las Vegas Motor Speedway

LAS VEGAS, NEVADA

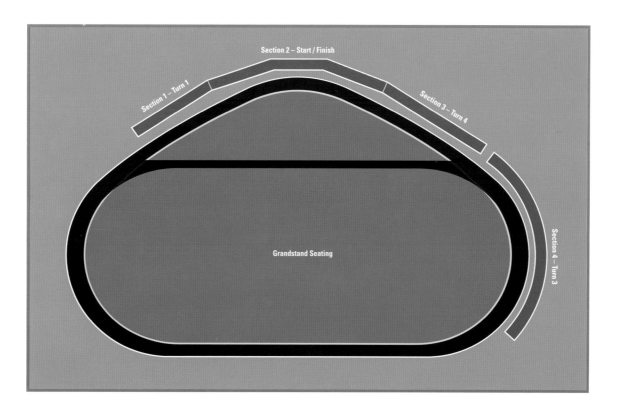

Section 2 – Start / Finish

Section 1 – Turn 1

Section 3 – Turn 4

Section 4 – Turn 3

Grandstand Seating

This low-banked, fully lit speedway situated just north of the Las Vegas glitter already had a NASCAR history before it first welcomed the sanctioning body's "big league" in the spring of 1998. When the Winston Cup racers did arrive for the inaugural 300-mile event, the track became the 164th—and the newest—facility to host the division.

Although the event and the facility were new, it did not mark the first time the circuit had raced in the state—or in the city. That distinction had gone to a scheduled 200-mile race on a one-mile dirt oval known as Las Vegas Speedway Park in 1955, some 43 years before. It was run on the same day (Oct. 16, 1955) that Alfred "Speedy" Thompson was driving to victory in a 100-mile event at Martinsville, Va. (In the 1950s, it wasn't uncommon for two races to be held the same day. One in the East and one in the West. Both awarded points toward the same Grand National championship, which became the Winston Cup of today.)

Missouri's Lloyd Dane had put a '55 Mercury on the pole at 74.518 mph and led the first five laps ever contested by the circuit in the state. He gave way to the potent white Kiekhaefer-owner Chrysler wielded by Norm Nelson and fell by the wayside in the early going. Nelson, of Wisconsin, kept the lead through a lengthy red flag and was still ahead of the field when the race was called short after 111 of 200 laps scheduled because of darkness. He held a two-lap advantage when the race was stopped. Both Thompson at Martinsville and Nelson at Las Vegas were driving Chrysler 300s owned by Mercury Outboard Engines' Kiekhaefer to give the irascible owner two victories on the same day—one in each half of the country.

Although the Winston Cup stars wouldn't return to Las Vegas until they arrived at the new 1.5 mile D-shaped oval in 1998, other NASCAR divisions had already tested the facility. The first stock cars to race there were NASCAR's Winston West circuit in November 1996 with Winston Cup regular Ken Schrader emerging as the track's inaugural winner. The next day, Jack Sprague, driving a Rick Hendrick-owned Chevy pickup, rode to victory over Bill Elliott at the final event of the NASCAR Craftsman Truck series' inaugural season.

Both the Winston West and Truck events saw racers battling two and three abreast all the way around the track, despite speeds that approached 160 mph. Both races were run at night under the track's state-of-the-art lighting system, which make it possible for the first time to hold events in that state without suffering through the notoriously

TRACK TACTICS

Wide and smooth, it takes a strong engine and drafting ability to win here. Tire pressure, shock, and spring selections are the keys to success. Three-abreast racing may be a norm at this desert-ringed track.

high daytime temperatures.

In March 1997, the track made history as the site of the first NASCAR Busch Grand National Series race ever run west of the Mississippi. Kentucky's Jeff Green piloted a Chevrolet to the win with a 2.8-second margin over veteran Dick Trickle. But it was not an easy victory. Green had to make the last of 25 lead changes among a dozen drivers. The 200-lap race, as well as the previous day's NASCAR Southwest Tour 133-lapper, again saw drivers battling three abreast for position throughout the field and throughout the races. The smattering of Winston Cup drivers who participated in the events were excited about their division's 1998 newest arrival.

The facility, sitting 17 miles northeast of the famous Las Vegas Strip at I-15's Exit 54, is a privately built racing complex. In addition to the mile-and-a-half oval, there is a half-mile dirt track, a drag strip, and 2.5-mile road course and a three-eighths-of-a-mile paved oval plus motocross and go-kart tracks.

Veteran racers on the new track and their fans had already listed the Las Vegas Motor Speedway among the most perfectly designed and most raceable facilities on the circuit. After attending their race on the track in 1998, the drivers of the Winston Cup's division concurred.

Mark Martin, inaugural winner of the Las Vegas 400, poses with his trophy, flanked by glittering showgirls, March 1, 1998.

Bill Elliott's #94 car in the pits during the Las Vegas 400, March 1, 1998.

The pack on its first pace lap at the beginning of the Pennzoil 400 on November 14, 1999.

Homestead-Miami Speedway

HOMESTEAD, FLORIDA

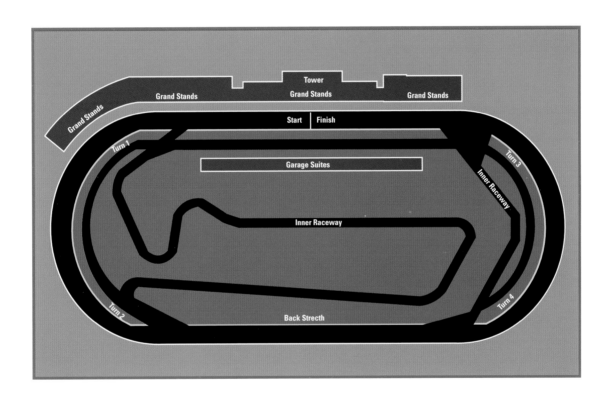

When this South Florida 1.5-mile track hosted its first Winston Cup race in November 1999, it had a trio of distinctions among its peers: It immediately became the southernmost facility in the nation; it was the largest of the five tracks that are truly oval in shape; and it was the only facility of such design—equal and parallel straights and turns of the same radius and banking—among the five 1.5-mile tracks that host the sport's top division. (The Atlanta track lost its claim to the latter two when it was redesigned to a truncated tri-oval, à la Charlotte, in 1997.) The track maintained its third distinction

in 2001 when the 1.5-mile Chicago and Kansas tracks joined the circuit as two more tri-ovals.

The NASCAR banner first waved over the site's palm-studded landscape in 1995, when the track hosted a trio of races featuring the Goody's Dash, Craftsman Truck, and Busch Grand National series, even though the truck event was an "exhibition race" before the popular pick-ups became a point-awarding circuit. At that time, the track was a "quad oval" with four distinct turns, looking like a smaller version of Indianapolis. The track proved to be competitive—all three of the races concluded with the top three machines crashing in

The oval's low banking and sweeping turns places the emphasis on each team's shock and spring selection, along with tire-management throughout the race.

the final laps. Dexter Canipe became the track's first NASCAR winner when the top three cars in the Dash race wrecked in the third corner. The trucks wound up the same way, with Geoff Bodine driving through a final lap melee to take the checkered flag, and Dale Jarrett got by the spinning top three cars in the Busch event to become the winner of that 300-mile chase.

The track was created to boost the sagging south Florida economy, which had been devastated by Hurricane Andrew and the closure of Homestead Air Force Base. The local officials realized a major motorsports complex could attract visitors to the area and bolster the revenues derived from the sun worshipers who annually crowd the beaches along the Atlantic. The site is just a few miles south of the two-mile Broward Speedway, where in February 1949 Bill France presented a ten mile "Novice" race for new cars. It was the introduction of the series now known as

Winston Cup. (The first actual race was held in Charlotte, North Carolina, in June of that year.) The track's layout had been changed by the time the Winston Cup cars and stars raced at Homestead for the first time in November 1999. The four corners had been replaced by sweeping six degree banked turns on either end of the 1,760-foot, three degree banked straights.

Time trials for the inaugural Winston Cup event here resulted in former Busch Series champion David Green earning his first pole in the sport's major league, with a lap of 155.759 mph to top the 43-car field. On raceday, the Kentuckian proved his speed lap was not a fluke by becoming the driver to lead the first lap of Winston Cup competition. Another Kentucky native, three time Cup champion Darrell Waltrip, earned distinction on the other end of the spectrum as a mishandling car caused him to withdraw from the race after just 85 laps, making him the

Left: Elton Sawyer spins during the Busch series Miami 300 on November 12, 2000. Sawyer was not injured in the crash.

Right: Tony Stewart, left, showers Bobby Labonte as they celebrate after the Pennzoil 400 on November 12, 2000. Though Stewart won the race, Labonte finished fourth to clinch his first Winston Cup title.

first driver out of the race.

Green held the lead for the first seven of the 267 laps that would be contested under the southern sun of the Sunshine State. In the eighth lap of the race, John Andretti, driving for owner Richard Petty, created the event's initial lead change as he passed Green for first place. It would be the first of 19 exchanges of command among ten different drivers that afternoon. Four of the lead swaps occurred between Joe Gibbs' teammates Bobby Labonte and Tony Stewart. Although the younger Labonte brother led the most laps that day, it was his teammate who fronted the field for the final 11 circuits and went on to a 5.2-second victory margin over Labonte and the six other cars on the lead lap at the end. It was the third victory of Stewart's rookie season, a record for a freshman driver. The eight lead lap cars were part of the 39 still in competition in a race that saw only one display of the yellow caution flag, that for oil on the track. The minimal number of caution laps allowed Stewart to record the track record pace of 140.335 mph for the 400 miles.

Stewart's race-speed record remained unbroken when the circuit returned in 2000, but the winner of the second annual edition was not disappointed. Stewart's repeat win in 2000 came at a slower pace, but was just as satisfying, as it came in the first event ever televised nationally flag-to-flag on NBC. It also afforded him the distinction of being only the second driver to win the first two races at any of today's Winston Cup tracks, thus joining only "The King" Richard Petty who won the circuit's first two races at Dover in 1969 and 1970.

Dale Jarrett, winner of the track's opening Busch event four years earlier, finished fifth in the track's first Winston Cup event, but that was good enough to wrap up his first driving crown. His winning that championship made the Jarrett family the second in the division's history to have two generations with the elusive crown. Dale's father, Ned Jarrett, was twice a champion of the circuit in the 1960s. They joined only Lee and Richard Petty in the accomplishment.

159

Bobby Labonte (left) and Tony Stewart wave to the crowd on November 12, 2000, after Stewart won the race and Labonte sewed up the Winston Cup title.

Chicagoland opened its gates to NASCA with a Busch race, the Hills Bros. 300, on July 14, 2001.

Chicagoland Speedway

JOLIET, ILLINOIS

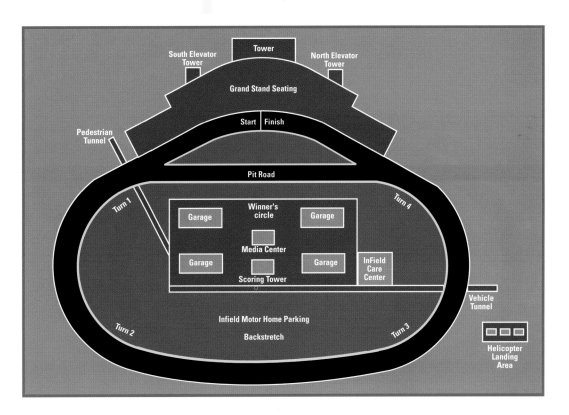

Forty-five summers passed without a NASCAR Winston Cup race in the Chicago area. In July 1956, Fireball Roberts drove a Pete DePaolo Ford to victory in a 200-lap chase, defeating a 25-car field at a half-mile oval in historic Soldier Field.

Two years earlier racing's major leaguers had raced in the state for the first time. That event was a 100-mile battle on the half-mile dirt track at Willow Springs, a Chicago suburb, with Dick Rathmann piloting a Hudson Hornet to victory.

In July 2001, the Winston Cup Series returned to the area at a new 1.5-mile state of the art facility on a 930-acre site. For a little perspective on the size, the Chicagoland Speedway's infield is large enough to hold four Soldier Fields, home of the famed Chicago Bears, and the site could accommodate 42 United Centers, where Chicago's Bulls and Black Hawks vie. The track's sweeping turns greeted the NASCAR stars with 18 degrees of banking—the same banking found in the tri-oval at Daytona or in the turns at the two-mile tri-oval in Michigan. The banking in the middle of the arcing front stretch tilts at 11 degrees. But the track's unique feature, unlike any other on the circuit, is the bowed backstretch. Banked at five-degrees (for drainage), the 55-foot wide stretch makes a continuous arc

TRACK TACTICS

The bowed backstretch allows more speed entering the third turn. Rear gear selection can prevent engine over revving.

from the exit of turn two to the entrance of turn three. Although the track is now the sixth to feature the mile-and-a-half configuration, it is the only track where there is no point on the racing surface where the car is going straight. (The only other track with that feature was Langhorne Speedway in Pennsylvania, a one-mile circle, where they raced from 1949 through 1957).

Actually situated on the edge of the Chicago area in Joliet, Illinois, the track opened by hosting a NASCAR double header for the Busch Grand National and Winston Cup Divisions. The curtain raiser was a 300-mile race on Saturday featuring the Busch battlers. Their 43-car field was led to the initial green flag by pole winner Ryan Newman, who had posted a speed of 181.866 mph. It would be Newman, in a Roger Penske-owned Ford, who would lead the first lap of NASCAR competition on the track. He led 26 laps before the first of six lead changes occurred and Jimmy Spencer took command of the event. The final swap of the lead came in the 158th circuit, when sophomore driver Jimmy Johnson put his Chevrolet into first place. It was a position he never relinquished—he went on to a 4.9-second victory margin over Mike Skinner and the rest of the field, for the first victory of his NASCAR career and the first win at Chicagoland Speedway.

The next day, Sunday, July 14, 2001, the Winston Cup brigade made ready to compete on the 167th track in their history. The 43-car contingent was led to the starting

flag by Todd Bodine, the youngest of the racing Bodine brothers of Chemung, NY. His pole winning effort, the first of the 2001 season, had come at a tempo of 183.717 mph, and he fronted the field for the opening six laps. At that point, the first lead change in the division's history at the track came when veteran Ricky Rudd got around Bodine's car.

Thirteen changes among eight other leaders ensued, with the final taking place in the 242nd of the 267 laps. At that point rookie Kevin Harvick passed Mark Martin to lead the final 26 circuits and take a .649-second victory. It was the second Winston Cup triumph of his career, and it came just 16 races after being tapped by owner Richard Childress to succeed legend Dale Earnhardt, who had lost his life in a last-lap-crash in the season-opening Daytona 500. (Harvick's first win came at Atlanta earlier in the season.) Seventeen of the 34 cars running at the end of the race were on the lead lap with Harvick, who saw his pace slowed ten times during the afternoon by yellow flags.

The victory allowed Harvick to not only strengthen his grip on Rookie of the Year honors, but also to inscribe his name in the annals of NASCAR racing history as an inaugural winner at the track, alongside Johnny Mantz at Darlington, Lee Petty at Daytona, Fireball Roberts at Atlanta, and Richard Petty at Dover. Harvick, however, might have an asterisk by his name as the only rookie to win an inaugural race.

Ken Schrader follows the pack into the third turn during the Tropicana 400 in July 2001.

162

Kevin Harvick leads the Tropicana 400 on July 15, 2001. He became the track's inaugural winner.

Jeff Gordon takes a practice lap around Kansas Speedway on opening day, September 27, 2001.

Kansas Speedway

KANSAS CITY, KANSAS

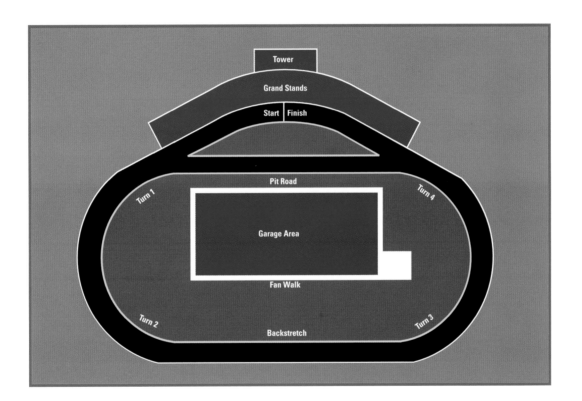

The Winston Cup Series had competed for 53 years before it presented its first race in Kansas. Their arrival at the new 1.5-mile Kansas Speedway in September 2001 confirmed the track as the 168th to host an event for stock car racing's major league. It also marked the Breadbasket of America as the 36th state to host an event for the division since the first race was held in June 1949 at a dusty three-quarter mile oval in Charlotte, North Carolina.

The sparkling new facility was the seventh on the 2001 schedule listed at a mile and a half in length. But, like all of its peers, it had its own personality and characteristics. The two main turns were banked at a unique 15 degrees. The front stretch with the start-finish line in the middle of the arced tri-oval is banked to a 10.4-degree angle and the 2,207-foot-long back straight is the lengthiest among all of the 1.5-mile tracks, nearly four football fields longer than the next closest.

Built and owned by International Speedway Corporation, it became a sister facility to Daytona, Talladega, Miami, California, Darlington, and the other ISC tracks. The track took four and one third years to complete, from the planning stage in 1996 to the inaugural ARCA and Winston West double-header in early June 2001. The construction required movement of 11 million cubic yards of dirt (enough to fill five NFL stadiums). Frank Kimmel, the defending ARCA champion, crossed boundaries to win the track's opening NASCAR Winston West event while Jason Jarrett, son of NASCAR champion Dale Jarrett and grandson of two time NASCAR series champion Ned Jarrett, scored his first major career victory by taking the ARCA event later the same day, June 2.

The open-wheel cars of the Championship Auto Racing Teams (CART) further tested the track's logistics and facilities the following month to set the scene for NASCAR's Busch Grand National and Winston Cup teams' arrival at the end of September.

Over $5 million was up for grabs in the September 29-30 double-header, and a strong field of Busch and Winston Cup teams were on hand to go for their share in the respective events. First up was the Busch contingent that found Vermont's Kevin Lepage taking pole honors for the Busch Series' 300-mile chase with a lap of 174.210 mph. But race day saw Winston Cup and Indy car veteran Robbie Gordon lead the first lap and the next 29 before Lepage could get back to the front of the field. They were just the first two of seven drivers who swapped the lead a total of eight times. The last lead change came in the 172nd lap of the 200 circuits in contention. That was when defending series champion Jeff Green took a command he never let go of. He crossed the finish line with a two-second edge over runner-up Hank Parker, Jr.

The uniqueness of the track's design proved a difficult adjustment to some. A dozen of the 43 cars that started were idled when Green scored his fourth victo

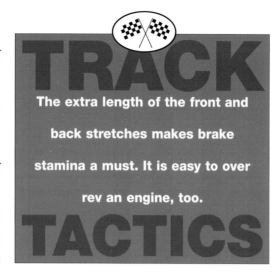

ry of the season. Half of those who failed to finish were sidelined by accidents.

Inaugural pole honors for Winston Cup went to a surprising rookie candidate, Jason Leffler, as he topped the field with a lap of 176.499 to score the first pole of his Winston Cup career. He narrowly nosed out veteran Jeff Gordon as the track's top qualifier for the first Winston Cup race in the state. In a Chip Ganassi-owned Dodge, Leffler led the 43-car field throughout the initial eight circuits of the 167 laps in the race. The first lead change was found in the ninth lap when Jeff Gordon, already the winner of inaugural events at Indianapolis and California, became the track's second Winston Cup lap leader and creator of the first of 19 lead changes for the day. After the capacity crowd of 75,000 watched a dozen drivers lead the race, and 13 caution flags attested to the track's degree of difficulty, it was Gordon's Chevrolet leading the way to the checkered flag to score his third win in a track's inaugural Winston Cup race.

The track's modern amenities belied a treacherous nature. Just 30 of the 43 cars that took the starting flag were still around when Gordon led the way to the checkered silk. Of the 13 that failed to finish, ten had been taken out by accident, with the first coming in the opening lap when rookie Casey Atwood hit the solid retaining wall.

The state's first race for the NASCAR stars was such a success it sent track officials heading for the planning board to move ahead with the second phase of construction, doubling the seating to 150,000, big enough to accommodate the population of the Virgin Islands.

A capacity crowd of 75,000 watched the first Winston Cup race on September 30, 2001.

Before the inaugural race began, fans participated in a special tribute to America after the devistation of September 11, 2001.

Dale Earnhardt holds the series championship trophy in victory lane at the North Carolina Motor Speedway on October 24, 1994.

T "Looking Ahead to the Future"

Through the preceding pages we have examined the sport and uniqueness of the tracks that afford it a showcase for intense competition. Each of the latter presents a different challenge to the drivers and teams. No two are the same. We trust the words and pictures have enhanced your understanding and appreciation. But, as important as it may be to examine the tracks' history and variables, it is equally vital that we use this knowledge to look ahead at the future of the sport.

The Loss of a Legend

NASCAR's Winston Cup circuit entered the twenty-first century and its fifty-third season of competition with a bright outlook. With a new multi-year, multi-million dollar television package in hand, continuing interest and fan growth, and heading into two new major markets with new facilities, the season opening 2001 Daytona 500 was a pivotal point. In it, the sport found a new winner when Michael Waltrip made his initial trip to a victory lane. But, as the exuberant Waltrip headed for the checkered flag, his car owner and mentor, Dale Earnhardt, died in a last lap crash while holding third place. He missed the joy of seeing two of the cars he owned, driven by Waltrip and his son Dale Junior, battle for the final few yards for a victory in the sport's biggest race.

Dale Earnhardt was an icon of the sport. He was its seven-time champion, a winner in seventy-six races on all kinds of tracks—super speedway, inter-

mediate, short tracks, and road courses. He won more races at Daytona Speedway than anyone, and he'd won a record $41 million during his stellar Winston Cup career, the most by any driver in any form of motorsports on earth. Of equal importance was the fact that he was the personification of a professional stock car driver. He was tough and talented, skilled in both driving a car and working on it. A second-generation race driver, he honed his skills on the dirt tracks of the Carolinas and adapted them to prowess on paved tracks.

Ironically, Earnhardt's death was the first to occur in either of Daytona's major races, the 500 or summer 400. His passing left a huge hole, one that will be hard to, and may never be, filled for fans, his fellow competitors, and the officials of stock car racing.

But his death, the twenty-ninth in all the testing, practice, qualifying, and competitive races over the sport's fifty-three years, brought a heightened focus on safety. From it we feel

Dale in the Winner's Circle at the Brickyard 400 in August 1995.

improvements will come to the cars and equipment that can reduce the danger to other drivers in a sport that carries inherent risks by its nature. Previous fatalities have led to improved helmets, better roll cages, enhanced driver retention systems, fuel cells, window nets, better brakes, stronger suspension systems, and the inner liners in tires. Earnhardt's loss led NASCAR to establish a new research and development department to investigate accidents and recommend safety improvements for the competitors, cars, and tracks.

Facing Foreign-Car Phobias

Other twenty-first century aspects of the sport may lie in the brands of cars fans will see competing before them, whether seated in the grandstand or viewing them on television at home. The NASCAR rules call for the vehicles to be "American-made steel-bodied passenger sedans." In today's world, Chevrolets and Fords are built in Canada or Mexico, while Honda and Toyota have factories in the United States. There is foreign ownership of companies that make many U.S. cars and American ownership of "foreign" makes. You see more Mercedes, Hondas, and Toyotas on the roads of our cities and states. We don't feel it will be too long before some of those makes will be competing against the Fords and Chevrolets. The tracks described in the previous pages of this book have long been the testing, development, and promotional arenas for Detroit and Dearborn. Can the same use be far off for the kinds of cars so many Americans now drive?

Fitting in More Fans and More Events

Some of today's tracks, notably Darlington, Bristol, Rockingham, and Darlington, were fortunate to have been built when they were and allowed to grow with the sport. All are situated in small demographic-index markets. Locations in similar areas would not be considered now for a race date, much less two, with the present desire for new major markets by the sanctioning body, series, and team sponsors. Many feel the trend will be to reduce the number of races at such tracks to one annual event and open the other date to events in larger markets in other areas of the nation. We have noticed the new tracks

introduced to the circuit over the last decade are granted just one event a season, a trend we feel will continue.

We notice, too, a national trend away from taxpayers' willingness to be extorted by professional sports for new public-funded facilities under the threat of moving the team to another city. Virtually all of the tracks described herein were built and are expanded and maintained by private funds. If tracks need more corporate suites and seating, the tracks build them without going into the public coffers. Civic leaders have noted that the arenas, stadiums, and coliseums are predominantly filled by fans who drive from their homes to the stadium, park, go in and watch the game, then get back in their cars and return home with little economic input in the community. But race fans at the major events are mostly from outside the area of the track, travel great distances, buy gas, stay in motels, eat in area restaurants, and pour millions of dollars of new money into the economy of the area.

The Homestead-Miami track has been a boon to the South Florida area that had been devastated by a hurricane and closing of a military base. The return of Winston Cup to the economically depressed Watkins Glen region of New York has helped salvage its business environment. As a result of this awareness, we may see future tracks afforded the same economic "perks" and support that have been offered previously to "stick and ball" team owners.

The look ahead through the windshield of Winston Cup racing is bright. There may be slick spots on the way into the future, and there are certain to be growing pains, but the sport and business of stock car racing will keep roaring ahead into the twenty-first century.

Dale and Teresa Earnhardt celebrate after the #3 car won the Winston 500 at Taladega, October 15, 2000, and Dale secured the one million dollar bonus. It was his final victory.

CLOCKWISE FROM TOP LEFT: Dale shares a moment with his son, Dale Earnhardt, Jr.; Dale jokes with his friend, Darrell Waltrip;
one of many memorials in front of Dale Earnhardt, Inc., headquarters in Mooresville, North Carolina; a two-tire pit stop prior to Dale's victory at the 1998 Daytona 500.

Cars snaking through S-turns at Sears Point, 1997.

Acknowledgments

No project of this scope occurs without the cooperation and assistance of many.
To each of them I offer my gratitude and appreciation.

Thanks first to my late mother, Lois, who helped inspire an appetite for stock car racing when she brought my brothers
and me from England to America and settled us in Daytona. It was she who allowed us to sell programs and work in concession
stands there and who let us hitchhike to Darlington for the first races on the first super speedway. My thanks to my brothers,
Mike and Andy, who slogged with me through the soft beach sands laden with programs, and to the teachers at
Seabreeze High in Daytona, who armed my mind with knowledge and an appreciation of history. A special thanks to the late
Don O'Reilly, my first boss at NASCAR, and the late Houston Lawing, my guide and tutor at Daytona International Speedway's
publicity department, both of whom shared their love of the sport and great work ethics with a fledgling.

This effort could not be possible without my wife, Skimp, who has made this journey through the sport with me
and has been an unpaid coworker and contributor through much of it. Through this work we hope our grandchildren
can learn more about the sport their grandfather has been proud to be a part of for more than a half-century.

I must also acknowledge the concept and detail efforts of Mary McGuire Ruggiero at Running Press, who has guided
the book to fruition. I am also appreciative of the outstanding input from Jonathan V. Mauk, Director of Daytona Racing
Archives, and to the past and present public relations directors at all of the tracks presented in these pages.

Finally, I extend my thanks and the appreciation of stock car racing's fans to the men who made the sport possible by
providing, without burden to their area's taxpayers, the facilities where the best drivers in stock car racing have raced.

Stock car racing, at this, its highest level, is a team endeavor. Likewise, this book required the efforts
of many to relay this body of information and images to you, the reader.

Cars streak around the track at Kansas Speedway.

Winston Cup Track Mailing Addresses

ATLANTA MOTOR SPEEDWAY
P.O. Box 500
Hampton, GA 30228
(770) 946-4211

BRISTOL MOTOR SPEEDWAY
P.O. Box 3966
Bristol, TN 37625
(423) 764-6555

CALIFORNIA SPEEDWAY
9300 Cherry Avenue
Fontana, CA 92335
(800) 944-7223

CHARLOTTE MOTOR SPEEDWAY
P.O. Box 600
Concord, NC 28026
(704) 455-3200

CHICAGOLAND SPEEDWAY
P.O. Box 3339
Joliet, IL 60434
(815) 727-7223

DARLINGTON RACEWAY
P.O. Box 500
Darlington, SC 29532
(803) 395-8499

**DAYTONA INTERNATIONAL
SPEEDWAY**
P.O. Box 2801
Daytona Beach, FL 32120
(904) 253-7223

**DOVER DOWNS
INTERNATIONAL SPEEDWAY**
P.O. Box 843
Dover, DE 19903
(800) 441-7223

HOMESTEAD-MIAMI SPEEDWAY
One Speedway Boulevard
Homestead, Florida 33035
(305) 230-RACE (7223)

INDIANAPOLIS MOTOR SPEEDWAY
4790 W. 16th St
Indianapolis, IN 46222
(317) 481-8500

KANSAS SPEEDWAY
13330 Meadowlark Ln, Suite 201
Kansas City, KS 66102
(913) 328-7223

LAS VEGAS MOTOR SPEEDWAY
7000 Las Vegas Blvd, N.
Las Vegas, NV 89115
(702) 644-4443

Rookie Kevin Harvick in the Winner's Circle at Chicagoland, July 15, 2001.

MARTINSVILLE SPEEDWAY
P.O. Box 3311
Martinsville, VA 24115
(540) 956-3151

MICHIGAN SPEEDWAY
12626 U.S. Highway 12
Brooklyn, MI 49230
(800) 354-1010

**NEW HAMPSHIRE
INTERNATIONAL SPEEDWAY**
P.O. Box 7888
Loudon, NH 03301
(603) 783-4931

NORTH CAROLINA SPEEDWAY
P.O. Box 500
Rockingham, NC 28380
(910) 582-2861

**PHOENIX INTERNATIONAL
RACEWAY**
1313 N. Second St., #1300
Phoenix, AZ 85004
(602) 252-2227

**POCONO INTERNATIONAL
RACEWAY**
P.O. Box 500
Long Pond, PA 18334
(800) RACEWAY

**RICHMOND INTERNATIONAL
RACEWAY**
P.O. Box 9257
Richmond, VA 23227
(804) 345-7223

SEARS POINT RACEWAY
Highways 37 & 121
Sonoma, CA 95476
(800) 870-7223

TALLADEGA SUPERSPEEDWAY
P.O. Box 777
Talladega, AL 35161
(205) 362-7223

TEXAS MOTOR SPEEDWAY
P.O. Box 500
Fort Worth, TX 76101
(817) 215-8500

WATKINS GLEN
2790 Conty Rt. 16
Watkins Glen, NY 14891
(607) 535-2486

Photography Credits

AP/Wide World Photos: pp. 24 (left), 43, 46, 52, 55, 58, 60–62, 67, 72, 86, 91,111
   (top), 112, 124, 128, 131–132, 134–136, 142, 148, 151, 156, 158–159, 164,
   168–171

Atlanta Motor Speedway Staff: p. 88

Courtesy of California Speedway: pp. 150, 176

Courtesy of Charlotte Motor Speedway: pp. 82, 83 (left), 85

Courtesy of Chicagoland Speedway: pp. 160, 162–163, 175

CIA/Bristol Motor Speedway photo by Ernest Masche: p. 92

Brian Czobat: back flap

Greg Crisp: pp. 3, 6, 9–17, 19 (top), 20–21, 23, 24 (right), 25, 38–40,
   66, 68, 74, 78–80, 83 (right), 84, 96, 99, 102, 105, 118, 121, 123, 137, 172

© James Cutler: pp. 106, 108–109, 111 (bottom)

Daytona Racing Archives: pp. 8, 26–34, 36–37, 42 (left), 48, 50–51, 54, 56–57,
   70, 73, 76–77, 89–90, 95, 98, 114–117

Tom Donoghue: pp. 152, 154–155

© Duomo/Corbis: cover photo

Sandy Hoerner, Racing Connection©: p. 19 (bottom)

Courtesy of Kansas Speedway: pp. 166–167, 173–174

Nigel Kinrade: pp. 64, 69

Collection of Buz McKim: p. 49

Courtesy of Martinsville Speedway: pp. 42 (right), 44–45

Courtesy of North Carolina Speedway: p. 101

Courtesy of North Carolina Speedway/Chobat: p. 100

John Owens/NHIS: pp. 138, 140–141

Photo by PIR/Tim Rempe: p. 126

Phoenix International Raceway: p. 127

© R. N. Masser/Pocono International Raceway Archives: p. 122 (left)

© Pocono International Raceway Archives: pp. 120, 122 (right)

© Frank Primrose: p. 143

Private Collection: p. 63

Courtesy of Texas Motor Speedway: pp. 144, 147

ABOVE: Sunset at the California Speedway, Fontana, California.